The Machine Embroidery Handbook

The Machine Embroidery Handbook

Designing Fabrics with Stitching, Manipulation, & Color

dj Bennett

Lark Books
Asheville, North Carolina

**To our grandchildren, Elliot, Dustin, Annie, and Molly,
the next generation of creative spirits**

Editor: Carol Parks
Art and Production: Kathleen Holmes
Photography: dj Bennett
Illustrations: Bernadette Wolf
Editorial assistance: Valerie Anderson, Laura Dover Doran

Library of Congress Cataloging-in-Publication Data
Bennett, Dj.
    The machine embroidery handbook : designing fabrics with stitching,
manipulation, & color / dj Bennett.—1st ed.
        p.   cm.
    ISBN 1-887374-45-0
    1. Embroidery, Machine.   I. Title
TT772.B4597   1997
746.44'028--dc21   97-13888
                                                              CIP

10 9 8 7 6 5 4 3 2 1
First Edition

Published by Lark Books
50 College Street
Asheville, North Carolina 28801, USA

© 1997 dj Bennett

Distributed by Random House, Inc., in the United States, Canada,
   the United Kingdom, Europe, and Asia

Distributed in Australia by Capricorn Link (Australia) Pty Ltd.,
   P.O. Box 6651, Baulkham Hills Business Centre, NSW 2153

Distributed in New Zealand by Tandem Press Ltd., 2 Rugby Rd.,
   Birkenhead, Auckland

THE PHOTOGRAPH ON PAGE 3 SHOWS A CUFF DETAIL
FROM THE STOLE ON PAGE 46. ON PAGE 5, AT LEFT,
IS A DETAIL FROM THE BOOK COVER *FIRE AND ICE*,
DESCRIBED ON PAGE 70. THE DETAIL AT RIGHT IS
FROM MOLLY'S QUILT, PAGE 120.

CONTENTS

THE FABRIC OF CHANGE

CHANGE IS THE ONE TRUE constant in our fast-moving times, and certainly occurs in the world of fabrics. This book deals with it in two different ways: fabric, in the larger sense—the make-up, nature, and essence of change; and in the literal sense—actual fabric, the materials we use to demonstrate this change.

Machine embroidery involves an exciting relationship between fabrics and threads, and the stitches that relate them to each other. Imagination is the catalyst that makes this relationship vital.

FIGURE 1. COMPLEMENTARY COLOR SCHEMES ARE DRAMATIC.

In the past 10 or 15 years, many new materials have become available. Fiber artists have expanded their interests to include plastics, metallics, ceramics, weaving, and sculpture. New machines and new needles have broadened stitchers' horizons. This book expands traditional concepts by examining this wealth of new materials: it uses basic techniques in unexpected combinations and opens avenues of experimentation. That's what creative machine embroidery is all about.

My own work has changed over the years as I have explored these new materials and different ways of using them. Constance Howard, that very important lady of English embroidery, once said that any creative embroiderer should weave his own fabric. At the time I was a bit skeptical—she had access to the extensive equipment of one of London's prestigious art colleges where weaving one's own fabric was a bit easier than in the ordinary stitcher's studio or home. But now I think I more fully understand what she was saying. I find myself creating new fabrics though my embroidery. There is less emphasis

on variety of stitches; greater emphasis on varying the use of simple stitches and techniques. There are fewer lines of demarkation between embroidery and fabric and closer affinity between fabrics and threads, to the point where there is very little distinction between the two. Indeed, I am creating new fabrics through embroidery.

This book is the result of my own experimentation since 1980, when *Machine Embroidery with Style* was published. At the end of that book I said, "In conclusion, this is only the beginning." And I feel that strongly. With this book as with that one, I hope to encourage experimental stitchers to explore broader aspects of the field. This is done through discussion, illustrations, and problems posed to challenge your ideas and creative expression. With you I share successes and difficulties—I have experienced them too!

Fortunately, there is no *complete* book of machine embroidery. Direction and inspiration can continue to lead to new and exciting discoveries in the future.

HOW TO USE THIS BOOK

The information in this book is presented sequentially, each technique building upon the previous ones. It is assumed that the stitcher has some experience with the basic stitch techniques that are used—these are reviewed on pages 10-12. The emphasis is less on the technical aspects of stitching and more on combinations of disparate materials and techniques.

Background material and explanatory text introduce each new technique. Then you will be asked to experiment with the technique by making a series of samplers. These are designed to give you a broader view of each concept and to inspire further independent exploration on your part. In each section are photographs of pieces that show how each technique can be used in a variety of ways. No two stitchers will interpret these exercises in the same way. This is good! You are encouraged to develop your own individual style, and to attain results that are uniquely yours.

Even though you have some experience in machine embroidery, you will derive the maximum benefit from this book if you will work through it from beginning to end. Most techniques and concepts build upon the preceding ones in a conscious, constructive way. The book does not lend itself to "dip and do."

KEEP A NOTEBOOK

The samplers you create as you experiment with the techniques in the book will provide you with a comprehensive reference source for further exploration and for finished embroideries. If you teach, you will have in effect stitched your own textbook, one to which additions can be made and from which new ideas will spring. You will have a ready reference of teaching aids.

Develop an organized method of handling the samplers. Most are adaptable to a standard notebook, 8½ by 11 inches (21½ by 28 cm). Finish the edges of each piece neatly with a zigzag stitch or with a serger. Slip the sampler into a protective plastic sleeve of the kind used in photo albums, and insert it in a ring binder.

On a sheet of paper, make note of materials used and add your comments about the exercise. Place this into the plastic sleeve at the back of each sampler.

At the end of each exercise you will find questions and suggestions for analyzing the sampler you have created. Establish the habit of questioning and assessing your own results. Your notes will help you plan future projects. If you plan to teach, your own experiences will be valuable in communicating with your students. Through working your way into difficult situations and out of them, through honest self-criticism, you can better understand students' problems and help them find their own solutions.

COLOR THEORY AND COMPOSITION

Color and composition are as important to good design as the stitching itself, and both aspects are stressed as part of the experimentation with each new technique. The photographs in each section illustrate not only examples of the technique itself, but the interaction of the design elements.

Before you begin to work with the techniques, take time to review the characteristics of good composition; all are important to creating a successful piece of embroidery. Following are the six elements with which we design.

Line has been described as "taking a dot for a walk." Machine embroidery is particularly adapted to splendid linear variety.

Area results whenever a line is closed. It creates shape and provides definition (fig. 2).

Color is one of the most exciting elements of design. The primary colors are red, yellow, and blue; the secondary colors—orange, green, and violet—result from a mixture of the primaries on either side of the hue. Study a good color wheel, a magical thing in itself, and play with the various combinations that work together.

Certain color schemes are recognized as basic ones. *Monochromatic* color schemes involve tints and shades (values) of a single hue, an elegant and subtle scheme. A *tone* is a hue to which another hue has been added to form a value or color change. An *analogous* scheme involves colors side by side on the color wheel and should include only one dominant primary. The result is an exciting, richly glowing effect. A *complementary* scheme (fig.1) involves colors directly opposite each other on the wheel. This color scheme is dramatic, particularly if one hue dominates and only a tiny touch of the opposite hue is used. If equal amounts are used, vibration and an "op" effect result.

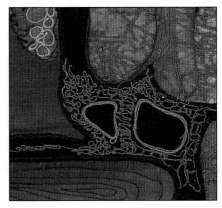

Value, mentioned in connection with color, is the fourth element of composition. It denotes the lightness or darkness of a hue. Value can add strength and dramatic impact to a composition.

FIGURE 2. A CLOSED LINE BECOMES AREA.

Texture refers to the surface feel of a piece, whether is it rough or smooth, hard or soft, matte or shiny, and so on. Texture is an especially important consideration when working with a variety of textiles as we will be doing.

Volume refers to third dimension and can be either actual or implied. Actual volume can be achieved by building up very high textures through fabric and thread manipulation or padding, forming an embroidery in the round, or by using some other means to elevate the usually flat surface of the fabric.

The second kind of volume is implied. A feeling of third dimension on a two-dimensional surface is suggested through chiaroscuro, change of scale, value changes, or any other means of creating the illusion of an object existing in space.

A good composition consists of certain characteristics, all important to the overall design.

Variety is achieved by a conscious and intelligent use of the elements mentioned above.

Unity adds strength and a feeling of comfort to a composition.

A recognizable **focal point** is desirable: it provides dramatic impact and adds to the interest of a piece.

A pleasing relationship between **positive and negative areas** is important. Both the positive, or stitched, areas and negative, or unstitched ones, contribute equally to the success of a composition (fig. 3). Too often a designer will concentrate so much on the stitches and threads that the negative fabric areas are ignored. These should be as interesting and varied as the stitched ones. Developing awareness of these elements and characteristics, and how to make best use of them, is one of the most important aspects of creative embroidery. It comes only through lots of experience and careful assessment of your completed piece.

FIGURE 3. POSITIVE/NEGATIVE RELATIONSHIP IN LACE

THE SEWING MACHINE: AN EXTENSION OF YOUR HAND

When I teach, I am often asked about the machine I use, and what kind I would recommend for embroiderers in the market for a new one. And I've discovered some stitchers collect machines like most stitchers collect fabrics and threads! I have yet to find the ideal machine, one that includes all the desirable features. Instead, the following list describes machine features that are absolutely essential for an embroiderer (number 1) to those that are merely very handy (numbers 11 and 12).

1. Power and durability. Embroidery is demanding on a machine. It should be constructed of heavy metal (some fiberglass or nylon gears are acceptable) and have a sturdy, powerful motor.

2. Third arm. This is a knee control that raises and lowers the presser foot, leaving both hands free to control the fabric and to move freely from place to place in the composition.

3. Distance between needle and the upright of the machine body. A distance of 7¼ inches (18.5 cm) is required to move a 12-inch (30.5-cm) hoop freely in all directions without striking the upright.

4. Knob controls for stitch width adjustment. Much of machine embroidery necessitates keeping the eye on the fabric while running the machine and changing stitch widths; this is possible only if the right hand can grip a knob and gradually make those nuances of change so necessary to advanced stitchery. Buttons and levers do not allow for this gradual transition.

5. Feed dog teeth that can be lowered. Most techniques in this book call for free machining, or free-motion stitching, where fabric is fed through the machine manually rather than by the teeth. If the machine requires a plate to cover the teeth, the machine bed is uneven and free machining is more difficult.

6. Removable bobbin case. The bobbin should be easily accessible so that lower thread tension can be adjusted or bypassed altogether. If you do a great deal of stitching with heavier thread, it is a good idea to invest in a second bobbin case just for the purpose. The original can then be kept in adjustment for regular sewing.

7. Ease in threading. We change threads often, and although practice makes for fast threading, some machines are much easier to thread than others. Ideally, threading should be a one-handed operation.

8. Zipper foot that allows very close stitching to edges. There is considerable difference among machines in how close one can stitch to an edge (such as a metal ring) with the zipper foot.

9. Inside access. The amount of stitching and variety of threads and fabrics used for embroidery create a great deal of lint and clutter, and it is an advantage to be able to get inside the machine to clean and oil it frequently. This is not possible on many of the latest sealed machine bodies.

10. Wide zigzag stitch. Most of the new machines have a wide swing of the needle, which is great.

11. Short shank. A short shank, when the presser foot is removed, allows the shank to pass freely over the hoop edge, eliminating the necessity of either tipping the hoop or notching it.

12. Capability of stopping with the needle either up or down. If the machine can be set to stop with the needle in the down position, both hands can be kept on the work at all times.

And finally, for those brilliant engineers who design sewing machines and who might just happen to peruse this book, I have my special wish list. First, **a continuous-feed bobbin:** what bliss to hook up the bobbin in such a way that it would feed continuously, yard after yard, from a large spool of thread. Next, a **transparent, spring-shank embroidery foot:** a small circular one that will not obscure or distort the view of what is being stitched.

MATERIALS AND TOOLS

The following tools and supplies will be needed for most of the samplers. At the beginning of each chapter there will be a list of additional supplies to be used in those exercises. Read the information on each exercise carefully, interpret it in the individual framework of your own experience, and then let your imagination soar! Try to expand your horizons a bit more with each sampler you work. And above all, have fun with it!

Your machine. Have it cleaned, oiled, and in good working condition. Keep the manual at hand for ready reference.

Presser feet. In addition to the regular zigzag foot you will sometimes need the spring-shank darning foot, an open-toed foot, a pintuck foot, and the zipper foot.

Needles. Have a good supply of standard universal-point needles, sizes 80/12 and 90/14 of the type required for your machine. You will also need a spring needle, which has a tiny plastic foot and a plastic top connected by a small spring. It is extremely helpful anywhere that extra surface stabilization is needed. It can also be used in some cases in place of the hoop. It

cannot be used with a presser foot or when working closely around found objects, beads, or buttons.

Some exercises will call for a double needle. These are sized according to the amount of space between the needles as well as by needle diameter. Take care when using a double needle with any stitch that has a side-to-side motion that the needles don't strike the stitch plate or presser foot. Check first by walking through one complete stitch sequence.

Although machine embroidery doesn't require any other special needles, there are several made specifically for use with certain threads, such as metallic and rayon. If you have difficulties with specialty threads, ask your machine dealer whether there is a special needle that might be helpful.

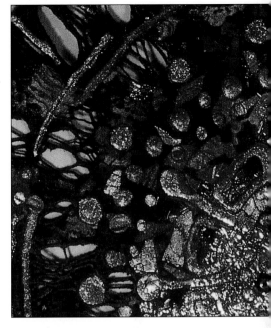

FIGURE 4. *BRÜNNHILDE'S SHIELD,* A HIGHLY TEXTURED DETAIL.

Hoops. Best are wooden hoops, 8 and 10 inches (20 and 25.5 cm) in diameter, or 12 inches (30.5 cm) for large pieces. It pays to buy good quality. They should have a screw-type adjustment and be narrow enough to fit under the presser foot shank with the foot removed. Wind the inner section of each hoop with twill tape or strips of muslin for better contact. Plastic hoops will not work except where a 3- or 4-inch (7.5- to 10-cm) area is involved. Plastic bends and gives, preventing proper fabric tension.

Fabrics. You will need an assortment of cottons and polyester/cotton blends. Many of the techniques will call for additional fabrics.

Threads. Almost any kind of machine thread works for embroidery—cotton, polyester, cotton-wrapped polyester, metallics, and monofilaments. Have on hand an assortment of colors. For couching, try a variety of heavier yarns and novelty threads.

Notions. You will need shears and thread snips, and 2-inch (5-cm) quilters' pins with ball tops. Some of the techniques will call for additional notions.

STITCHING TECHNIQUES

The exercises throughout the book involve using the stitching techniques described below. Free machining, or free-motion stitching is the basic technique upon which the other stitches are built. If you have never tried it, practice until the motion feels completely comfortable to you and you have good control of the stitching.

Machine embroidery involves imaginative use of basic skills. Technically there is only one stitch possible on the machine—a loop stitch, formed when the top thread makes contact in the bobbin race with the bottom thread, resulting in a stitch that lies flat along the top and bottom surfaces of the fabric. There are a number of variations possible, some of which commonly are referred to as "stitches."

These variations can result from directional change of the needle, as for a zigzag stitch; the stitch length as altered by motion of the fabric, as for the creation of knots and blobs; the stitch width, accomplished by manual adjustment of the machine or variation in the relationship between swing of the needle and direction of fabric motion; and textural differences caused by tension changes, as in the whip and cable stitches. Further variations are possible through use of the limitless variety of fabrics and threads available to the imaginative stitcher. The combinations of all these possibilities are the subject of this book.

FREE-MACHINE EMBROIDERY

Also known as *free-motion stitching or free machining*, this technique involves lowering the feed dog teeth, removing the presser foot, and feeding the fabric manually through the machine. It is a very mobile, creative way to stitch since it permits complete control of stitch length and direction.

Use a standard needle and ordinary sewing thread, and set the stitch width for straight stitching. Stitch length does not signify since the teeth are dropped. You will control it through the movement of the hoop.

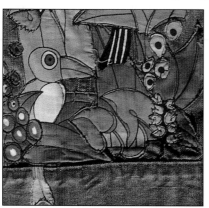

FIGURE 5. APPLIQUÉ WITH FREE-MOTION STITCHING

Frame the fabric, drumhead-taut, in a wooden, screw-adjusted embroidery hoop. Wrap the inner hoop with twill tape or muslin strips for better contact with the fabric. Use the hoop in an upside down position in contrast to that for hand embroidery, with the fabric against the bed of the machine. Place the outer rim of the hoop on a firm surface, place the fabric on it, and seat the tape-wound inner rim of the hoop. Grasp the excess fabric with thumbs and fingers and rotate and *push* toward the center of the hoop, gently and firmly tightening as you move around the circle. Tighten the screw if possible, and firm up again. Tap the fabric—it should sound like a drumhead. If the fabric is not framed tightly enough, the thread will break when you stitch.

Caution: Make certain the presser foot lever is down when you stitch even though the presser foot is removed; this lever also controls the upper thread tension. When you thread the machine the lever should be up.

Free-motion stitching takes some practice in order to find the right balance of machine speed with motion of the hoop. It is best to run the machine fairly fast to prevent the needle from catching in the fabric and breaking against the sole plate. The hoop may be moved at almost any speed. Practice writing your name—it's a familiar motion. Then try stitching with the stitch width set for zigzag. Remember, there's a direct relationship between practice and results!

KNOTS AND BLOBS

These textural changes in the stitching are formed by keeping the fabric stationary while stitching. For knots, use a straight stitch setting, and for blobs, a zigzag setting. Knots will resemble the small French knots of hand embroidery. Knots can be heightened by using whipstitch (below). For a multicolored effect, try contrasting top and bobbin thread colors.

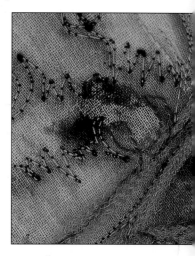

FIGURE 6. KNOTS ARE FORMED AT TOPS AND BOTTOMS OF WHIPSTITCHED LINES.

WHIPSTITCH

This so-called "stitch" occurs when there is tension difference between top and bobbin threads. When the top tension is greater than the bobbin, the bobbin thread whips up around the top thread, creating a slightly textured, almost beaded kind of line (fig. 6). If different colors are used top and bottom, a multicolored stitch results. By varying the difference in tension (tightening the top, loosening the bottom), different effects are created. Extreme differences in tension can result in the bottom thread completely covering the top. The creative stitcher controls this variation to add interesting color and textural effects. Experiment with both straight stitch and zigzag. Try using whipstitch for knots and blobs.

A word of caution: The tension adjustment screw on the bobbin case is very short. Hold the case over a box lid while adjusting tension so the screw won't be lost if it comes out.

CABLE STITCH

This stitch involves tension change, but for a different reason than in the whip. Here the embroidery is worked from the wrong side and heavier thread is used in the bobbin. Heavier threads increase the bobbin tension, so bobbin tension should be set looser than normal to allow the heavy thread to pass through. Very heavy threads such as single-ply Persian wool or number 3 pearl cotton, might have to bypass the tension spring altogether (fig 7).

Since we are working from the reverse side of the fabric, these heavier bobbin threads will lie on the surface of the piece. Lovely, loopy textures result from experimenting with different weights of threads and different concentration of stitches. Use normal tension on top for this stitch. Experiment with both straight and zigzag stitches.

FREE-MACHINE QUILTING

Quilting occurs when stitching changes the contour of a "sandwich" of two pieces of fabric with some form of batting or padding between them. Each time a stitch is worked, this changed surface reacts to light in a different way, enhancing and enriching the surface of the fabric.

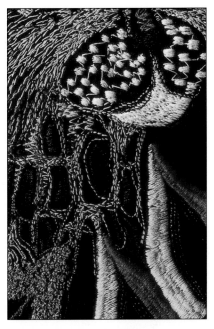

FIGURE 8. WHIPSTITCH WAS USED FOR THE CAT'S FACE, CABLE FOR THE PEBBLY FILLING AT LOWER LEFT AND BLOBS FOR THE WHITE DOTS AROUND THE NOSE.

A hoop is not usually necessary for machine quilting, but with free machining some sort of stabilization is necessary. A spring needle or a spring-shank presser foot—a darning foot—provides stabilization and allows for freedom of movement. Machine quilting is stronger than hand quilting, an advantage in garment-making. It produces a linear appearance slightly different from the traditional beaded, up-and-down texture of hand quilting. Use a slightly relaxed top tension for quilting, but experiment first because tension setting will vary with type and weight of fabrics used.

Use heavier weight fabric for the base since the padding rises toward the least resistant fabric. A lighter weight fabric on top reacts beautifully to the loft or raised contour. Both straight and zigzag stitches can be used. For an interesting stippled effect, add knots, concentrating them at pleasing intervals.

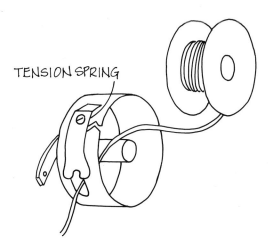

TENSION SPRING

FIGURE 7. BYPASSING THE BOBBIN CASE TENSION

FIGURE 9. FREE-MACHINE, OR FREE-MOTION, QUILTING

COUCHING

This is a delightful technique that allows for lots of imaginative experimentation. It involves two threads. One is laid on the surface of the framed fabric, the second (the machine thread) is used to fasten it down, or couch it.

When couching is worked with feed dog teeth up and a presser foot in place, a hoop is not necessary. Free machining will require framing in the hoop. Many different threads, ribbons, and strips of fabrics that can't go through a machine can be used as laid threads for couching.

Experimentation is encouraged here. Straight stitch, zigzag, and pattern stitches all can be used. Set a blind hem stitch to catch only the edge of one side of a soft, thick laid thread for an unusual textural effect. Play with different ways of tying down that laid thread. Tie knots in the laid thread, ravel it, string beads on it— the possibilities are endless.

Use your own good sense with regard to stabilizing the fabric. The laid thread can be pinned to the ground fabric. A presser foot and teeth can be used, eliminating the need for a hoop, but free machining is more mobile and more fun. With free-motion couching, use a spring needle or spring-shank foot for stabilization. I often use a bare needle and stabilize the stitching with a broken pencil or cuticle stick held just in front of the needle as the stitching progresses. This allows for very creative manipulation of the laid thread during stitching besides providing the necessary stabilization of fabric and threads.

■

A BEGINNING SAMPLER

A PERSONAL ASSESSMENT

Before exploring the techniques covered in the rest of the book, assess the skills you have acquired up till now. These may have come from past courses, exploration, observing work of contemporary artists in the field, and reading.

List all "stitches" and their variants which you feel comfortable using. Make a second list of techniques such as applique, couching, quilting, etc., and combine all of them in a well-planned embroidery no smaller than 8 by 11 inches (20 by 28 cm). Before you begin, review the elements of good design and take into consideration such things as an effective focal point and the overall unity of the piece. Remember, since you will be combining so many stitches and techniques in one piece, that careful selectivity is one of the most important aspects of designing. Use fabrics and threads of your choice. Choose any subject that appeals to you, objective or non-objective, and give your imagination full rein. Think and plan carefully, then have fun!

■

FIGURE 11. THE WELL-PREPARED STITCHER

FIGURE 10. THICK AND THIN YARNS COUCHED WITH STRAIGHT STITCH

APPLIQUÉ IS THE STITCHING of one fabric to the surface of another. Originally the technique must have developed from necessity. Early man probably attached one piece of skin to another to cover an arrow slit or knife cut in an animal skin used as a garment. Later on, woven whole cloth was tedious to make and was regarded as a precious commodity by the general population. Patches were used to prolong the life of what was perhaps an only garment. But somewhere along the line, some creative person noticed that certain patches added distinction and interest to a plain piece of fabric, and appliqué developed for aesthetic as well as functional purposes. We have been using it to good advantage ever since. Recently *The New York Times* fashion page featured the "new" hobo look, patches applied artistically to designer garments—a practice coming full circle for entirely different reasons!

Appliqué is quite compatible with machine embroidery, and for many people who use the machine, it is the only artistic expression they have the inclination to attempt. It is strong, bold, and colorful, but it can also be subtle; it gives one the opportunity to work with different textures and types of fabrics in one piece, and is one of the best methods for filling areas. Satin stitch filling, by contrast, is tedious, time-consuming, and requires more patience and technical skill.

We shall consider two basic types of appliqué here—flat and raised. Flat appliqué, the type most commonly used, involves cut-out pieces of fabric which lie flat on the surface of another and are held in place by some kind of finishing edge, usually a row of satin stitching. Raised appliqué, on the other hand, elevates the cut pieces above the surface of the ground fabric by means of some kind of padding placed between the two fabrics. This, in order to accommodate the raised contours, necessitates a slightly different handling of the edges. Interesting variations of both types of appliqué are possible, and it is with these variations that we are concerned.

MATERIALS

For the appliqué samplers described on the following pages you will need the the basic supplies listed on page 9. You will also need paper-backed fusible web; plastic food wrap; tulle; a small amount of padding, such as cotton or quilt batting.

FLAT APPLIQUÉ

For this type of appliqué it is best to use some adhesive to secure one fabric to the other. There are many products intended for use with appliqué; whichever you use, be sure to test it with your fabrics and follow the manufacturer's instructions for use.

An effective appliqué backing is paper-backed fusible web, marketed under several brand names. The paper backing makes shapes easy to cut, and the adhesive backing on the fabric shapes helps prevent fraying. The backing will stiffen the fabric only slightly. With less than the recommended pressing time, this material can be used to position appliqué pieces just temporarily for stitching.

The coated side of the material is ironed onto the wrong side of the fabric to be applied, then the design can be traced or drawn (in reverse) on the paper. The shapes can then be cut out and pressed in place on the ground fabric.

An alternative to the commercial materials is ordinary plastic food wrap. It is rather difficult to manage, but works well for temporary bonding. Place it carefully between the layers of fabric and fuse with a warm iron. The clingy plastic is tricky to cut to shape, and if it creeps out at the last minute, which it can easily do, it will gum up the sole plate of the iron.

Plastic wrap was used as the adhesive on *London Mews*, a long vest (fig.12), but here a small piece of plastic was placed in the center of the applied fabric with no attempt to follow the contours of the edges. This was enough to hold the shapes in place until the edges were finished (fig. 13). It is a simple and temporary staying device that comes in handy when nothing else is available. The wise stitcher should be familiar with both kinds of adhesives.

FIGURE 13. VEST DETAIL: APPLIQUÉ WITH HARD EDGE SATIN STITCHING

Equally important to imaginative appliqué is the stitching that finishes the edges. One of the main reasons for combining stitching with appliqué is to hold the fabric securely in place. For machine embroiderers, even more important is the aesthetic element the stitching provides. Traditional hand appliqué inevitably comes to mind—the edges of the applied fabric carefully turned under and anchored with tiny hidden blind stitching. Machine appliqué gives a somewhat different effect.

We're all familiar with the stock method of covering the raw edges of applied fabric with closely spaced satin stitch as shown in figure 14. Often there is no further variation than perhaps some tapered widths or mitered corners (fig. 16). This type of finishing is called a hard edge, and it can be very effective. It is precise, and neat. It provides a strong line of demarcation between applied and ground fabrics which is in keeping with the direct,

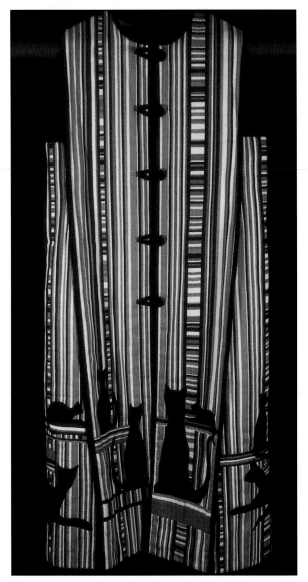

FIGURE 12. *LONDON MEWS*, A LONG REVERSIBLE VEST WITH APPLIQUÉ

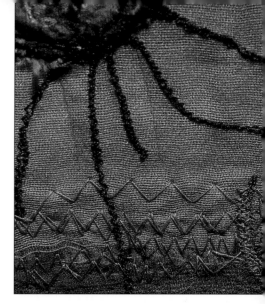

FIGURE 15. *THE FOUR SEASONS*, DETAIL. WIDELY SPACED ZIGZAG FORMS SOFT EDGE OF APPLIQUÉ.

FIGURE 14. *ELLIOT'S QUILT*, DETAIL. APPLIQUÉ EDGES ARE WORKED WITH SATIN STITCH FOR A HARD EDGE FINISH.

fabrics and thread colors. No matter if the applied edge frays slightly—that simply adds to the softness of the edge.

For a very harmonious finishing stitch, use a double needle with one thread to match the applied fabric and the other to match the ground. Be careful zigzagging with the double needle, however, as it cannot swing as far as the single without hitting the sole plate. Experiment with your machine first, determining what width of stitch will safely accommodate the double needle swing. In the example shown, stitching was done without a presser foot. A presser foot, if used, also must accommodate the swing of the double needle. Double needle stitches can be lengthened like the single needle zigzag to provide an even softer edge as described above.

child-like simplicity of both pieces. It can be varied through change of color, density of stitch spacing (stitch length), and width of the stitch.

The detail from *The Four Seasons* (fig. 15) shows a satin-stitched edge that has widely spaced long stitches suggestive of early spring grass thrusting above the earth's surface. This second type of finishing is called a soft edge. In this example, a wider spaced zigzag stitch creates the soft edge. The more widely spaced the zigzag stitches, the softer the edge becomes since it allows both applied and ground fabrics to show through between the stitches. The result is a gentler blending of

Soft edges can give a entirely new dimension to your technique. Soft edges are gentler, not so carefully defined, and add a great deal of variety and mobility to the overall effect.

Finished edges can be changed by varying their widths, adding grace and vitality to curved edges (fig. 16). The result is a vast improvement upon the old concept of making all finished edges the same width and weight.

FIGURE 16. TAPERED HARD EDGE SATIN STITCHING

Couching, too, gives edges a dimensional quality that can be used to good advantage in much appliqué work. Laid threads can be couched in such a way that the thread is compacted and depressed to produce quite a hard edge (fig.17), or they can be allowed to fluff and stand up above the surface of the fabric to create a much softer, more sensitive finishing (fig.18).

My favorite edge treatment is a series of straight-stitched lines, much like those one might draw with a pen. In the *Noah's Ark Vest*,

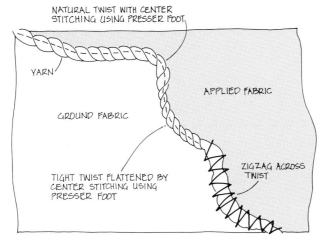

FIGURE 17. APPLIQUÉ WITH A COUCHED HARD EDGE

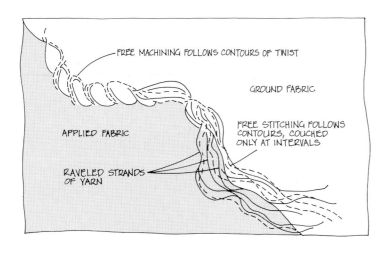

FIGURE 18. APPLIQUÉ WITH A COUCHED SOFT EDGE

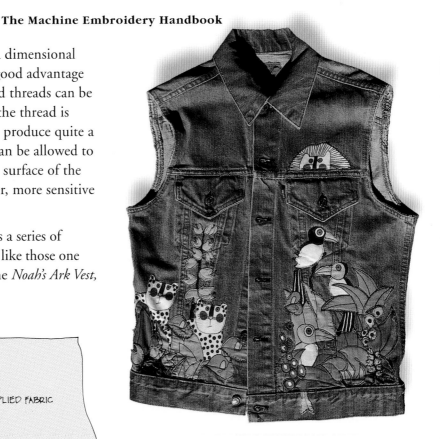

FIGURE 19. *NOAH'S ARK VEST.* **A VARIETY OF STRAIGHT-STITCHED LINES SECURE SOFT EDGE APPLIQUÉ.**

I "drew" over the applied edges with a variety of straight-stitched lines using free-motion machine settings and the spring needle (fig.19). If contrasting threads are used top and bottom, allowing for a varied whipstitch, a closer relationship between fabrics and threads can be achieved, particularly if the fabrics are multicolored prints. Whether a hoop is necessary depends upon the weight of the fabrics. Heavier fabrics, such as denim, need no more support than the spring needle. This type of finishing allows for a very close relationship between the applied areas and other areas of machine embroidery.

In all kinds of appliqué I feel it is extremely important to relate the stay stitching to other embroidery in the piece. I'm perfectly aware that some of the softer finishing methods offend those traditionalists who expect each edge to be solid, definitive, and neat; but for me, this variation of line allows for freedom and nuances of expression that can be attained by no other method. If there is danger of raveled edges (and use of a fusible backing minimizes this danger), several concentric lines of stitching will usually stay the edges as well as solid zigzag does. It is, after all, the basic nature of most fabric to be soft, so why not let a few edges ravel gently, adding another textural dimension to the whole?

There are times that a raveled edge best expresses the concept of the design—a soft, fluffy kitten, for instance, or willow trees blowing in the wind, or soft, summertime clouds—far better than a neat hard edge. As I suggested earlier, all depends upon the impression you wish to create in your embroidery. There is no one right or wrong way to do it.

The suggestions above are just a few ways that edges can be varied in appliqué. You will surely think of many more. The creative embroiderer takes advantage of the characteristics of both techniques and materials and learns how to make them work together.

■

Sampler 1
Flat Appliqué

Plan and stitch a piece involving flat appliqué with a variety of edge finishes, both hard and soft. Try both a commercial adhesive and plastic wrap. (Be careful not to allow the plastic to come in contact with the sole plate of your iron). Use both free-motion stitching and/or a presser foot to stay stitch the applied fabrics and to enhance and enrich the entire piece. Experiment with the spring needle with and without a hoop for the free-machined edges. Concentrate on relating the stitching to the overall concept of the composition. When the sampler is complete, finish the edges and place it in a plastic sleeve for your notebook.

Consider some of the joys—and the problems—you encountered in this experiment. Note the advantages or disadvantages of the different adhesives. What did you discover about the spring needle? Do you feel the contrast of hard and soft edges contribute positively to your piece? Slip these notes into the plastic sleeve behind your stitched sampler.

The *Noah's Ark Vest* (fig. 19) provided the opportunity to use a piece of commercially printed fabric that had been lying around my work table for quite some time. I cut it apart and rearranged the motifs, then applied them with both hard and soft edges. The vest itself was a castoff left in a closet after summer renters had departed. On the back of the vest was a very large motorcycle logo, and although I tried everything I could think of to remove the thing, it was there to stay. It simply had to be covered up. The ark served the purpose, although if you look closely you can still see the wingtips of the flying wheel logo in the curved prow and stern of the ark (fig. 20).

Traditional satin-stitched hard edges were used on the ark to give the effect of the solid wooden boards from which it was made. On the front, the lion peeking out over the top of the pocket illustrates how free-machine stay stitching can enhance the nature of the design, in this case the lion's shaggy mane.

FIGURE 20. DETAIL FROM VEST. HARD APPLIQUÉ EDGES SUIT THE WOODEN CONSTRUCTION OF THE ARK.

FIGURE 21. FREE-MACHINE ZIGZAG SUGGESTS THE LION'S SHAGGY MANE AND JAGGED LEAF EDGES.

The construction of the jacket was incorporated into the design, with the lion peering over the pocket at the yoke seam (fig 19). The detail (fig. 21) shows the jagged mane, leaf, and grass suggested by the stay stitching.

I feel that the softly frayed edges of the applied fabrics not only are in character with the grasses, cats' fur and leaves, but relate well to the casual nature of the denim garment, suitably worn and faded, with frayed armholes where sleeves have been cut away. I've worn this vest for a number of years now and have enjoyed every minute of it.

As you can see, edges become more than simply a functional device for holding one piece of fabric in place on another. They also can suggest different materials and qualities—an important concept in creative appliqué.

RAISED APPLIQUÉ

So far we have dealt primarily with line and area, the first two of the six elements of composition. Now let's address a third element: volume, or third dimension. There are two types of volume possible in stitchery. Implied volume creates the illusion of a third dimension on a flat surface through use of perspective, value change (shading), and change of scale. Actual volume, true three-dimensional effects, can be achieved with padding or some other means of raising the applied fabrics above the surface of the ground fabric.

In any type of padding or quilting, the applied fabric should be lighter in weight than the ground fabric for maximum loft. Padding pushes toward the area of least resistance.

A variety of materials can be used for padding—bits of quilt batting, cotton balls, or foam rubber all will work. Old nylon stockings make wonderful padding as well as top fabric for quilting. The padded areas can be further contoured with some simple stitching. Since nylons don't ravel they're ideal for soft edges, particularly since they can be rolled, stretched, and manipulated as you work, which adds to the spontaneity and verve of the whole.

To stitch padded appliqué, use free machining, spring needle, and hoop and/or use a presser foot with feed dogs up. If free-motion stitching is used to create soft edges, it is a good idea to use a hoop and spring needle.

In the sleeve detail of the jacket *Naiads Wear Green Sleeves,* rounded rectangles of suede cloth were applied without adhesive and with simple straight stitching. The stitching depressed the suede cloth enough that the centers rise up, creating the illusion of padding (fig. 22). This padded effect relates to the actual raised textures of heavy cable stitching and rows of raised loops stitched with the tailor tacking foot (see your machine manual for instructions).

FIGURE 22. A DETAIL FROM *NAIADS WEAR GREEN SLEEVES* SHOWS A RAISED PADDED EFFECT.

In *Annie Beth's Quilt* (fig. 23), the carousel ponies were padded. In a case like this, little if any adhesive is recommended. A small strip of adhesive can be applied to one edge of the appliqué, leaving the other edges free for stuffing. After stuffing, pin the free edges in place and finish as desired. As an alternative, pin the applied areas of fabric to the ground fabric, add the padding, then secure the pinned edges in the ways described above.

■

S A M P L E R   2

RAISED APPLIQUÉ, ACTUAL VOLUME

Lay out a composition of fabric shapes on a ground fabric, padding those shapes that will become the focal point of your piece. Make it a monochromatic color scheme, light in value, to realize the maximum effect of the contours created by the padding. Use both hard and soft edges, but this time use varied couching to create both edge types. You will find the spring needle works well for this, even if you are using a hoop, since it provides additional support for the laid threads as you couch. Use a pencil point to maneuver the laid threads as you stitch—it saves wear and tear on the fingers.

■

A more innovative method of raised appliqué with actual volume involves the use of sheer fabric—discarded nylons, net, or best of all, nylon or silk tulle. (Nylon is less expensive and works just as well.) With this method, applied fabrics, found objects, beads, all kinds of bits and pieces can be controlled under a layer of sheer fabric, which in turn can be manipulated and rearranged as the stay stitching progresses, providing a close relationship between stitching and fabric. This is a particularly free and inventive type of appliqué which I find relates beautifully to printed fabrics, batik, and textured surfaces (fig. 24).

FIGURE 23. *ANNIE BETH'S QUILT*, WITH PONIES IN RAISED APPLIQUÉ

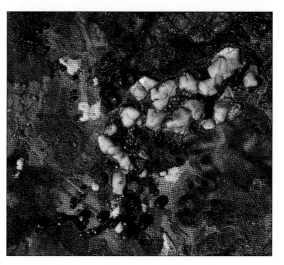

FIGURE 24. BEADS, PADDING, AND VARIETY THREADS ARE APPLIED UNDER SHEERS.

SAMPLER 3
RAISED APPLIQUÉ WITH FOUND OBJECTS

Place a ground fabric over the outer section of a hoop. Arrange the applied fabrics and small objects in the area, emphasizing a focal point, and place sheer fabric over the entire surface. Later, a long quilter's pin can be used to hold the small pieces in place for stitching. Place the inside hoop over this arrangement and carefully frame for free motion stitching. A variety of stitches can be used not only to secure the floating objects underneath, but to enhance the entire piece.

Objects can be moved, rearranged, and manipulated as the stitching progresses, resulting in an extremely free and spontaneous relationship between found objects and the stitching. Beads can simply be enclosed in a "cage" of fabric with stitching all around (fig. 26), but on a garment or other piece that will receive much wear and repeated laundering, each bead should eventually be stitched through to further secure it unless the bead hole is too small (fig. 25). The spring needle is excellent for this type of appliqué, but it will not work for stitching through bead holes as the spring prevents the needle from forming a complete downward stroke.

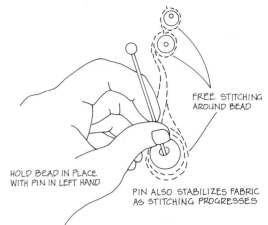

FREE STITCHING AROUND BEAD

HOLD BEAD IN PLACE WITH PIN IN LEFT HAND

PIN ALSO STABILIZES FABRIC AS STITCHING PROGRESSES

FIGURE 26. USE A QUILTER'S PIN TO HOLD BEADS FOR STITCHING.

Another way to secure beads, particularly those with holes too small to accommodate a machine needle, is to string them by hand with a beading needle and stitch down the stringing thread at intervals under the sheer. This is actually a form of couching.

Figure 27 shows a detail from a shirt that incorporates several of the techniques we've been discussing. It's a purchased shirt that I textured by wetting it thoroughly, then brushing on strokes of thin red, blue, and black acrylic paint (see Chapter 4, sampler 8). The paint ran and blended with the wet surface of the fabric to create subtle textures that relate nicely to stitching.

Two forms of appliqué were used. The pink and gray flower motifs were cut from an odd pillowcase from the five-and-dime. Paper-backed fusible web was applied to the wrong side, then selected motifs were cut from the fabric. It's usually easier to apply the adhesive before cutting the shapes since the adhesive supports the fabric and even controls bias edges that could otherwise wave or distort.

The floral motifs were arranged on the shirt, taking into consideration a focal point (for a figure like mine it is kinder to place it on the shoulder or close to the neckline rather than

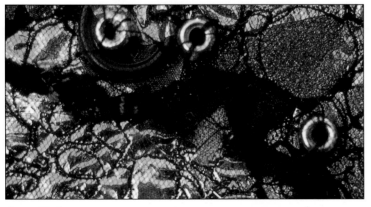

FIGURE 25. BEADS ARE ENCASED UNDER SHEERS AND LATER STITCHED THROUGH THE HOLES.

across the bust or in the center of the torso) and the overall movement of motifs around the neck, across the shoulders, and on the back. I feel very strongly that garments should be just as interesting from the back as from the front. Nothing discourages me more than to see an elaborately decorated shirt with absolutely nothing on the back. Remember, a garment is a complete composition that not only is seen from all angles, but that will move with the motion of your body. This adds an exciting dimension to the entire compositional challenge!

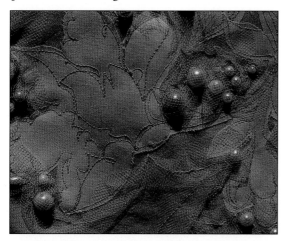

FIGURE 27. A DETAIL FROM A SHIRT SHOWS TWO KINDS OF APPLIQUÉ, WITH BEADS ENCASED UNDER STRIPS OF SHEER FABRIC.

A sleeve board was used to iron the motifs onto the shirt. It is a handy device when working around necklines and into shoulders and sleeves.

I decided to apply craft store "pearls" in a variety of sizes. The pearly white, gray, and soft pink colors related nicely to the colors in the printed fabric. I cut strips of pink tulle ¾ inch (2 cm) wide and manipulated them over and around the floral motifs, encasing the beads as I applied the tulle. Since the tulle doesn't ravel and is quite strong, it could be twisted, spread open, slit, and used doubled or tripled as cages for the beads (the holes in the beads were too small to accommodate the needle).

This was a garment to be worn, so I made sure that two or more layers of tulle were involved to strengthen the fabric cage around each bead. Some clusters of beads were grouped in larger cages, allowing them to move freely as the garment moved.

As I worked, I discovered the round bead had a maddening habit of squirting in the opposite direction just as I began to surround it with stitching. I found that a long quilting pin through the bead hole served as a handle to hold it in place temporarily until enough stitching was finished to secure the bead (fig. 26).

Long strands of tulle were taken vertically down the front and back of the garment, manipulated and turned to relate to the soft lines of paint. Rows of double-needle stitching were added (using a presser foot and feed dogs) to further emphasize the vertical lines that extended from the focal point toward the bottom of the garment. Double-needle stitching lines also moved down the sleeves to relate them to the more heavily stitched areas.

By this time you can see that most appliqué pieces actually combine several different techniques, all worked in conjunction with various types of free machining. With experience, you will learn which combinations work best in a given situation. The more you learn, the more choices you have, and the more selective you must be. Designing involves a great deal of decision making!

SAMPLER 4

SELECTIVE COMBINATIONS OF RAISED APPLIQUÉ

Plan and stitch a piece involving the various raised appliqué techniques described above. Be daring and experimental in your choice of materials. Concentrate on relating the stitching to the overall concept of the piece.

Experiment with various stitch textures that organically relate to the contouring of the appliqué.

What ideas does this sampler trigger for future experiments? Do you feel that some color/value schemes respond better to raised appliqué than others? Why? Did you encounter any problems?

■

The samplers from these exercises will provide you with ideas and valuable reference material, especially if you get in the habit of making notes on each piece, and jotting down comments about pleasures and problems encountered during the working of them. Place these notes on a separate piece of paper at the back of each sampler when it's mounted in its plastic sleeve. In this way you'll develop a meaningful working body of ideas for future use.

A sampler shouldn't be an end in itself—only a repository for current experiments and a springboard for future projects. The final test comes in using the techniques and ideas explored in the samplers.

I firmly believe that ideas are contagious. Sources for ideas are all about us—in nature, in man-made objects, and in the work of other stitchers. When I see an exciting piece of embroidery, I mull it around a bit mentally and combine it with the techniques I enjoy most. The result is an expression entirely different from the piece that provided the initial inspiration. Thus, throughout this chapter you will find examples of appliqué used in very different ways. I use it a great deal in garments, jewelry, wall panels—whatever stitching is taking place. These ideas are for you: study, analyze, add your own ideas and techniques—and create something entirely different from them.

Figure 22 shows a detail from my *Cat Skirt*. The motifs are from commercially printed fabric that was backed with fusible web before the cat shapes were cut. As noted previously, the adhesive with its paper backing adds body to the fabric and makes precise cutting easier. The cats were bonded to the ground fabric, front-facing cats on the front of the skirt and their back views on the skirt back. They were stitched in place (using a hoop) with linear free-motion stitching. The base line under the row of cats was finished with a solid row of satin stitching done with the embroidery foot and feed dogs up. Cat-shaped pewter buttons provide closures.

The ground fabric suggested to me the tawny stripes of the cats in the print. I feel there is a necessary close relationship between applied and ground fabrics. Here, stitching is kept to a minimum, quite in contrast to the pink and gray shirt (detail, fig. 27). There is a great deal of variety possible even when only a few simple techniques are used.

FIGURE 28. A DETAIL FROM THE *CAT SKIRT* SHOWS TWO TYPES OF APPLIQUÉ EDGE FINISHES.

FIGURE 29. APPLIQUÉ ELEMENTS ON A JACKET SLEEVE

Figure 29 shows the sleeve of a synthetic suede jacket. The fabrics are not pieced, but appliquéd. I was lucky enough to be given a bag of small scraps of the fabric, and it provided a fascinating challenge.

The jacket pattern was first marked onto a base of preshrunk cotton/polyester fabric. The scraps were positioned on the base without adhesive, each patch overlapped approximately ⅛ inch (3 mm). They were topstitched in place with a short zigzag stitch, using the satin stitch presser foot with the feed dogs up.

A word of caution is in order about embroidering on garments. Never cut out a garment piece until after the stitching is completed. Mark the pattern outline (I use chalk, then hand or machine stitch the chalk marks with a long basting stitch that is easily removed if necessary). On this garment, I extended the applied pieces beyond the pattern outline to compensate for the slight shrinkage that takes place with the stitching. After the embroidery/appliqué is finished, re-mark the pattern before cutting out, extending the applied pieces where necessary.

The sleeves of this garment were planned first so that a color sequence could be followed, moving from warm down to cool (there were fewer cool scraps). This sequence formed the focal point of the garment. The red fabric at the top of the photograph is the percale on which the pieces were applied. The main body of the jacket was limited to navy, black, beiges, and rusts. Threads were chosen to augment this color scheme.

As an additional surprise (which is always fun), and quite in contrast to the free, random appliqué of the outside, the lining is embroidered in a traditional, satin-stitched flower bouquet reminiscent of crewel embroidery (fig. 30). Hidden treasures, such as a bit

FIGURE 30. A HIDDEN TREASURE: EMBROIDERY ON THE JACKET LINING

Appliqué

FIGURE 31. *ELLIOT'S QUILT.* NOAH'S ARK AND ITS TRAVELERS

Figure 31 shows *Elliot's Quilt*, made for our first grandchild. The motif is Noah's ark, with figures cut from my husband's old shirts. The object here was to suggest child-like drawings; hence the stylized, simple shapes ideally suited to appliqué. Fabric crayons—another child-like suggestion—were used for the rainbow and some flowers. The border is simple patchwork.

Pieces of plastic wrap were used under the applied shapes to hold them in place temporarily, and most of the finishing was done in hard-edge satin stitching. The machine quilting was done free-form using a hoop and with the feed dogs down. Had I had access to the spring needle at that time it would have worked beautifully for the quilting, eliminating the need for a hoop.

Annie Beth's Quilt (fig. 23) was made for our third grandchild. The raised carousel pony figures were worked in a different way. Each horse shape was marked on fabric and roughly cut out with excess fabric all around to allow for framing in a hoop. Bridle and cinch strap were applied to the figures. Then I top-stitched each horse to a backing fabric with a narrow free-motion zigzag, following the outline of the horse and leaving an inch or so open for stuffing. The excess fabric was then trimmed just beyond the line of stitching, the horse was stuffed, and a narrow row of medium-length satin stitching was worked around the entire animal. Contouring details on the withers, jaw line, eyes and nose, etc., were stitched using a presser foot and with the feed dogs up.

Each figure was then backed with paper-backed fusible web. This time, contrary to previous suggestions, the adhesive was applied after the piece was cut out. Small bits and pieces were used to secure legs,

of very special embroidery on the lining of a jacket or some tiny treasure hidden within a "cave" of heavily textured stitches add a personal element that the casual observer will not see, but you, the artist, will know it is there!

head and tail; a larger piece for the body. The horses were ironed into place. Care was taken not to flatten the contours of the horse. The pieces were secured to the ground fabric with a slightly wider row of shorter satin stitching that covered the initial narrower row.

Notice that the procedures for the above two pieces are quite different from each other. This is part of the challenge of experimental stitching—working out the engineering of particular pieces. Often no two pieces present the same procedural problem; with experience, a stitcher learns to work this out in advance.

Ken's Patience (fig. 32) is a full-length coat that combines appliqué, quilting, and piecing. A small logo at the top of the lining was worked in crayon encaustic (see Chapter 4) and machine embroidery (fig. 33). Technically, piecing—the joining of related pieces of fabric to create a different one—is not embroidery. It falls in the crack between appliqué and fabric manipulation, which is discussed more thoroughly in Chapter 2. As mentioned above, however, special needs require special combinations of techniques.

The fabrics used in this coat were disparate and varied a great deal in texture and in weight. They include a heavy upholstery fabric, two upholstery-weight velvets, lightweight double knit, a cotton/polyester percale printed to resemble Amish quilt blocks, and fake fur with a double-knit backing.

The heavier fabrics could simply be pieced; the lighter-weight ones were applied to a base

FIGURE 32. THE COAT, *KEN'S PATIENCE*, INCLUDES A VARIETY OF PIECED AND APPLIQUÉD FABRICS.

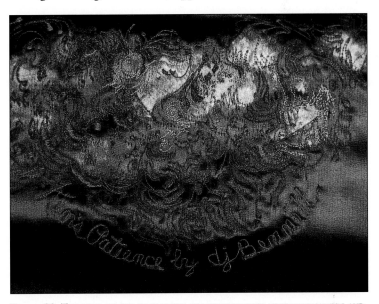

FIGURE 33. THE LOGO ON THE COAT LINING WAS WORKED WITH CRAYON ENCAUSTIC AND EMBROIDERY.

Appliqué

FIGURE 34. MUKLUKS, MADE OF FABRIC, FUR, AND LEATHER

FIGURE 35. MUKLUK DETAIL, CABLE STITCH USED TO SUGGEST BEADWORK

fabric before piecing. The printed percale was padded and quilted. Since the fake fur moved and crawled under the presser foot as it was being stitched, particular care was taken to pin-baste each piece firmly to the adjoining fabric before stitching.

The entire fabric collage was roughly laid out on the pattern, making sure that excess fabric was allowed for adjustments as the composition developed. Obviously this took a good deal of space. My husband, Ken, returning home after a long day at the office and hoping for a nap, asked a bit wistfully whether I realized every bed in the house was full of fabric. Hence the name of the coat.

While teaching in Canada several years ago I became fascinated with Eskimo mukluks, and their use of leather, fur, and beadwork. Could they be translated into machine embroidery? Certainly the leather could be applied by machine with a leather needle. The decorative bands of braid, fur, and leather strips could be attached the same way. What about the beads? The texture of the small seed beads reminded me of cable stitch filling. Figure 34 shows the completed mukluks. The cat design suggests the stylization associated with tribal art. Red leather is appliquéd to the ground fabric, a traditional felted wool, and finished with a hard edge of satin stitching (fig. 35). And, indeed, the cable stitch filling suggests the texture of seed beads. In addition to experiencing the satisfaction of working my way through a problem, I've worn these cozy mukluks with a great deal of pleasure!

Another form of footwear—leggings—is illustrated in figure 36. These were interesting to construct and are fun to wear. Although no appliqué was used on these particular pieces, it could just as well have been worked into the stitched design. I cut a muslin pattern to fit the contours of a pair of knee-high commercially made boots, allowing for a zipper down the back.

The embroidery (fig. 37) is primarily satin stitch (this is where the appliqué could have been used), cable stitch filling, whipstitch, and some blobs. Small tucks shape the leggings over the instep. Fabric straps are joined under the instep with hook and loop tape. Elastic gathers the top slightly to keep the leggings upright. They can be worn just as easily over ankle boots as with the taller ones, and are an unusual way to add dramatic impact to a simple costume.

I think you can begin to see that most embroidery does not involve just one method

FIGURE 37. DETAIL FROM BOOT COVER, SHOWING WHIPSTITCH, CABLE STITCH, AND BLOBS.

or technique, but rather is a harmonious and inventive combination of many. The larger your vocabulary of stitches and techniques becomes, the greater will be your ability to express yourself poetically with needle, fabrics, and threads. This is what advanced machine embroidery is all about.

FIGURE 36. PUSS ON BOOTS: EMBROIDERED BOOT

The London street markets hold a particular fascination for me. It has something to do, I'm sure, with the basic pack rat mentality that seems a vital part of every stitcher's make-up. One of our favorite markets is Camden Lock, situated alongside one of the numerous canals that cut through London. One summer while browsing alongside the canal we heard the sound of voices, first at a distance, then coming closer; rhythmic male voices chanting in unison, "Rape, pillage, and burn! Rape, pillage, and burn!" To our amazement, gliding from behind the warehouses lining that part of the canal came the familiar dragon-prowed longboat associated with the Vikings who invaded and explored England. Complete with round shields, swords, and horn-sprouting helmets, and obviously perspiring under the hairy animal skins they wore, four or five of the"Vikings" drew alongside the Camden dock and sprang ashore, swords in one hand, tin cans in the other,

soliciting donations for a children's hospital charity! In this chapter we shall do a bit of rape, pillage, and burning of our own, in a similarly important cause—creative use of fabric and threads.

Any type of embroidery involves changing the surface of a piece of fabric, sometimes to the extent of creating an entirely new one. Fabric can be changed through a variety of devices—stitching, distressing, folding, pleating, slashing, gathering, and other methods of manipulation. We shall work with some of these methods in this chapter. In Chapter 1 we explored different types of appliqué, and these methods can be combined with others in fabric manipulation. As you make these samplers, strive to incorporate techniques and methods of previous samplers into the current one whenever possible.

CUTTING, REARRANGING, AND MANIPULATING FABRIC

We are so accustomed to using only plain, solid-colored fabrics for embroidery that we often forget to explore the wonderful palette of printed fabrics available in today's fabric shops. Figure 38 and figure 27 show pieces of commercially printed fabric that have been cut out, rearranged, and applied to create new fabrics enhanced with simple machine embroidery.

MATERIALS
In addition to the basics described on page 9, you will need interesting, prewashed, printed fabric as well as pieces of plaids and checks. For best results, include four or five pieces of lightweight, 100 percent cotton and one piece of polyester/cotton double knit.

FIGURE 38. COMMERCIALLY PRINTED FABRIC CAN BE CUT OUT, REARRANGED, APPLIED, AND EMBROIDERED.

FABRIC REARRANGEMENT

Choose a piece of commercially printed fabric and analyze its design, color scheme, and general characteristics. Now create a new piece of fabric by cutting out elements of the design and rearranging them on a harmonious ground fabric. (See page 13 for information regarding adhesives to hold the pieces in place for stitching.) Use free-motion stitching in combination with other techniques of your choice. Keep in mind the principles of good design. Create a focal point, unity, and interesting movement. Above all, concentrate on relating the stitching to the organic feeling of the printed design.

Study your piece and determine whether or not you have improved upon the design of the original print. In what specific ways is it better (or worse)? In what ways have you related the stitching to the characteristics of the original printed piece? Does the focal point relate to the overall feeling of the piece while immediately attracting attention? What other devices might you have used to create this attention?

PIECING AND QUILTING

Cutting, rearranging, and seaming is another form of fabric manipulation that has been used for centuries and that can be used in conjunction with machine embroidery. The whole tradition of pieced quilts is based on this principle. From the simplest traditional nine-patch to the complex, curvilinear piecing of today's quilters, we can gain inspiration for further exploration. In Sampler 2 of Chapter 1 we worked with surface distortion of fabrics that involved primarily textural and/or pattern changes. Distortion can occur in shapes as well as textures and patterns.

FIGURE 39. AN INDONESIAN COAT OF PIECED IKAT FABRICS

Patchwork, in its simplest form, is the joining of pieces of fabric with hand or machine stitching. Not only is it a treasured American tradition among quilters since early colonial days, but it has even earlier origins in England, Europe, and Asia. Inventive stitchers down through history discovered the satisfaction of connecting bits of fabric in pleasing patterns of color and value when larger pieces of fabric were unavailable. Among early tribes, animal skins were pieced when shapes and sizes were inadequate for their desired garments, and the resulting outside seams were decorative as well as functional.

Although no proof is extant, I always imagine Joseph's coat of many colors as formed of patchwork. At any rate, the Bible suggests Joseph's coat was highly prized. A modern version might resemble the pieced ikat coat in figure 39.

Quite in contrast to that piecing, in figure 40 the dramatic yoke of a contemporary Hmong dress consists simply of narrow bands of colored fabrics seamed together in a form of strip piecing, where the raw edge of the first piece is covered by seaming the second to it. The multicolored triangles are versions of the prairie points (small, folded squares of fabric set into a seam) that quilters use to finish the edges of quilts (see fig. 52).

STRIP 2 STITCHED TO CENTER SQUARE (1) AND PRESSED OPEN

STRIP 3 PIECED SO AS TO COVER RAW EDGE OF STRIP 2

STRIPS 2 AND 3 PIECED TO 1, FOLDED OUT AND PRESSED FLAT

FIGURE 40. STRIP PIECING WITH INSERTED PRAIRIE POINTS

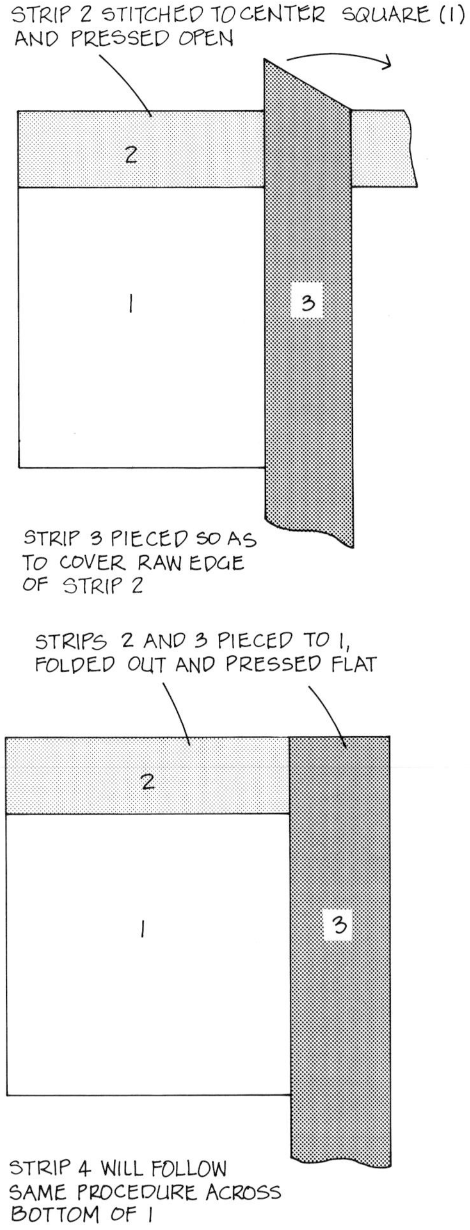

STRIP 4 WILL FOLLOW SAME PROCEDURE ACROSS BOTTOM OF 1

FIGURE 41. FOR A TRADITIONAL LOG CABIN QUILT BLOCK, ADD STRIPS IN EITHER A CLOCKWISE OR COUNTERCLOCKWISE DIRECTION AROUND THE CENTRAL RECTANGLE.

Strip piecing is a fundamental concept, one so simple that it is often overlooked as lacking potential for creative machine embroidery. The traditional log cabin quilt block is formed by piecing fabric strips of equal width clockwise or counter-clockwise around a square or rectangular center. Each added strip is placed so that it covers the raw end of the last, as illustrated. If the stripping is applied to a padded ground, it is known as the "quilt-as-you-go" technique.

During the 1970s and 1980s patchwork was taken to new heights of inventive application, especially in constructing exotic patterned garments. The reversible, strip-pieced vest shown in figure 42 involves joining strips of fabric to create more complex strips, which in turn are combined into a fairly complicated mosaic of fabric bits.

FIGURE 42. DETAIL OF A STRIP-PIECED REVERSIBLE VEST

The pieced suit, *Homage to the Amish*, figure 43, uses Amish fabrics and colors to create small elements of design (squares, triangles, rectangles) that are combined into larger strips for further piecing. The garment developed from the center outward in this fashion. In both the vest and the suit, patterns of color, values, and textures are played against each other in a carefully calculated composition.

Seminole patchwork (fig.44) is based on the same principle, but many contemporary pieces also depend upon a good deal of applied rickrack and bias strips for their patterns. Piecing can be used just to create beautiful patterns of strong color and value, but it is equally effective where subtle nuances of carefully chosen pastel color changes suggest the shimmering light of impressionist painters such as Constable and Turner.

And what has all this to do with machine embroidery? In its simplest form, patchwork combines fabrics and stitching, in our case machine stitching. One might question whether it is truly embroidery since no surface embellishment is involved. In my jacket,

FIGURE 43. *HOMAGE TO THE AMISH*, **A STRIP-PIECED SKIRT AND VEST**

FIGURE 44. DETAIL OF JACKET WORKED IN SEMINOLE PATCHWORK WITH RICKRACK ADDED.

Fabric Manipulation

31

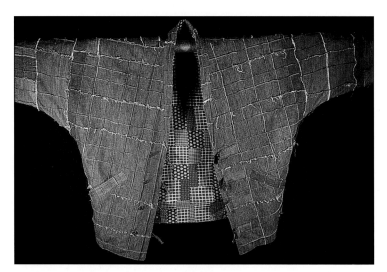

FIGURE 45. THIS REVERSIBLE JACKET BRIDGES THE GAP BETWEEN PIECING AND EMBROIDERY.

The Fine Line Between Piecing and Embroidery (fig. 45), I have attempted to bridge this gap. The jacket lining is hit-and-miss patchwork; the outside is random piecing of worn denim, with the seams on the outside (fig. 46). The soft, raveled edges of the fabric are stitched on the right side with the machine's built-in decorative stitches in a variety of colors, accented with tucks—hence the "fine line." This process can be as simple or as complex as the artist chooses to make it, and sometimes the most imaginative techniques can be overlooked because of their simplicity. It also can be combined with many other machine embroidery techniques.

In figure 47 the center of a traditional log cabin block is machine embroidered. In figure 48 a traditional quilt block (the cathedral window) forms the center of a log cabin block.

Piecing is usually associated with quilting, but as we've seen in most of the examples above, quilting is not a necessary accompaniment to piecing as there is no padding involved with those examples. Padding originally was used in early Chinese military garments, which were heavily padded and quilted for warmth and for protection against enemy arrows.

FIGURE 47. APPLIQUÉ AND MACHINE EMBROIDERY WERE USED FOR THE CENTER OF A LOG CABIN BLOCK.

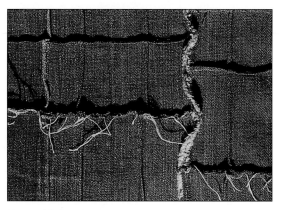

FIGURE 46. SEAM DETAIL OF THE JACKET SHOWN ABOVE

FIGURE 48. A TRADITIONAL CATHEDRAL WINDOW WAS USED AS THE CENTRAL SQUARE OF A LOG CABIN BLOCK.

Many contemporary garments eliminate that extra bulk unless it is desirable for warmth. From the practical standpoint, machine piecing and quilting has proven stronger and more durable than hand piecing, making it particularly practical for garments and accessories that would be laundered more often than quilts or wall panels. But from the purely aesthetic standpoint, quilting adds an elegant, embossed effect to the surface of the fabric which is quite special, and which provides the creative embroiderer with yet another opportunity for designing.

MATERIALS

For the next samplers you will need, in addition to the basics, some unbleached muslin, quilt batting, and a variety of fabrics for piecing. Prewash all fabrics.

■

SAMPLER 2
STRIP PIECING

This sampler involves strip piecing, its method, and ways in which it can be distorted, changed, and used in conjunction with machine embroidery. Strip piecing, as shown in figure 41, involves the placement of fabric strips around a central shape in such a way that the raw edges of the first strip are covered by seaming the next strip to it.

The log cabin block (fig. 49) is an example of this method. In both cases, the strips are built onto a central rectangle, and various color and value patterns are established using strips of the same width. In figure 50 the square of the strip-pieced log cabin block becomes a triangle (half-square) and the strips are added in a chevron pattern vertically from top to bottom rather than in the around-the-central-square motion shown in the drawing. Note too that strips are not of equal width, and that rickrack and stitching embellishes some of them.

Choose interesting fabrics in a color range that appeals to you, and with strong value differences. Some should be striped, some printed, some plain. The object of this exercise is to form a chevron-shaped panel of piecing in which the strips are varied in width, pattern, color, and value.

For the foundation fabric, cut a piece of muslin approximately 12 inches (30 cm) long and 10 inches (25 cm) wide upon which the stripping is built. With pencil or marking pen, mark a vertical line on the horizontal center of the piece. The piecing will result in uneven edges on all four sides, but don't worry about that—they will be cropped and trimmed to size after the piecing is finished. Cut half of a 4-inch (10-cm) square and pin or baste the triangle at the top of the vertical center, centering the long side of the triangle flush with the top and the point downward.

FIGURE 49. A STRIP-PIECED LOG CABIN QUILT BLOCK

Now the fun begins—constructing strips for a pieced chevron panel. Patchwork eats up fabric, particularly when you are working in a prescribed pattern, so make each strip 15 inches (38 cm) long. Vary the widths. Use ¼-inch (.7 cm) seams for the piecing, which means that each seam will consume ½ inch (1.4 cm) of fabric. Strips may be seamed together to create a wider strip of multicol-

FIGURE 50. CHEVRON STRIP PIECING IS A VARIATION OF THE LOG CABIN PATTERN.

ored, multi-patterned fabric. In other words, you are creating new fabrics to be used as elements in the stripping.

Experiment with directional changes in stripes. Notice in my sample (fig. 50) that in the top and bottom pairs of elements the stripes of the fabric run parallel with the seams. In the central pair of elements they run at right angles.

These elements can be enhanced with applied braids, laces, rickrack, ribbon, etc. Tucks and pintucking can be used to provide interesting textural changes. The machine's decorative stitches can be used effectively to alter the basic fabric. For additional variety, rows of buttonholes might be worked and ribbon threaded through them. Use your imagination, keeping in mind that the end result should be harmonious in color and pattern, and that eventually all these constructed strips will be pieced together to form a new fabric.

When you have constructed at least four 15-inch (38-cm) strips of varied combinations of color, value, and texture, fold each one end to end and cut into two strips (eight in total) for the chevron stripping. Decide which pairs of strips will be used first, second, third, etc. Position strip 1 of pair 1-2 right sides together along the right-slanting edge of the top triangle, allowing the strip to extend at least 2

inches (5 cm) beyond the top and bottom of the triangle. Be sure the long edges are precisely aligned. Use a presser foot and raise the feed dogs. Stitch the strip to the triangle with a ¼-inch (.7 cm) seam. Fold the strip down, away from the triangle, and press the seam flat. The pressing is extremely important to assure that the first strip lies properly.

Align strip 2 of the first pair, right sides together, along the left-slanting edge of the triangle so that it completely covers the raw central end of strip 1 and extends beyond the central line. Stitch, fold, and press as above. Repeat this process with the next pair of strips, aligning each one carefully so that the V of the resultant chevrons occurs along the central line on the muslin. Strip 3 of pair 3-4 should completely cover the raw end of strip 2. This will occur naturally if your elements are carefully measured and cut, and your seamlines are accurately stitched.

As you apply the pairs of strips you can see the new fabric appearing in a form completely changed from any one or all of the original fabrics with which you began. Trim uneven edges to page size and finish with a zigzag stitch or serger.

I hope you have begun to think of ways this technique can be used in your own needlework. The possibilities are vast. Figure 51 illustrates a composite use of strip piecing, fabric manipulation (manipulated tucks), and free-motion stitching in a reversible suit jacket. The jacket back (fig. 52) has a panel of chevron stripping seamed to a block of cathedral window surrounded by log cabin stripping, which is in turn seamed to a block of log cabin variant (more strip piecing), which all together form the central back panel. Strips are seamed out in both hori-

FIGURE 51. A REVERSIBLE PIECED JACKET, INNER SIDE OUT. A VIOLET MOTIF IS USED AT THE CENTER OF EACH SLEEVE BLOCK.

FIGURE 52. THE OUTER BACK OF THE JACKET. THE CATHEDRAL WINDOW PATTERN IS USED FOR THE CENTRAL SQUARE OF EACH LOG CABIN BLOCK.

zontal directions from this panel, including a strip of prairie points.

The sleeves are built from a basic log cabin block with a cathedral window center, topped with strips of tucks and prairie points. The reverse of the sleeve (fig.47) consists of two blocks of machine appliqué, leaves, and embroidered violets, surrounded by log cabin stripping. It is topped with a strip bordered with automatic pattern stitching.

The front of the suit skirt begins with a long central panel of irregular chevron strips which evolve in both directions into strips of manipulated tucks. The reverse of the skirt (fig.53) features a larger motif of the applied and embroidered violets and leaves, with stems extending to the bottom of the skirt.

Needless to say, by the time I engineered the reverse piecing and quilting of those panels I had pretty well worked strip piecing out of my system for some time to come! Happily, the garment is comfortable, personal, and a joy to wear. The first time I wore it traveling,

a flight attendant dumped a glass of orange juice into my lap, so I can also attest to its durability and washability.

In Sampler 2 the strip piecing was done without padding. In Sampler 3, we'll use batting

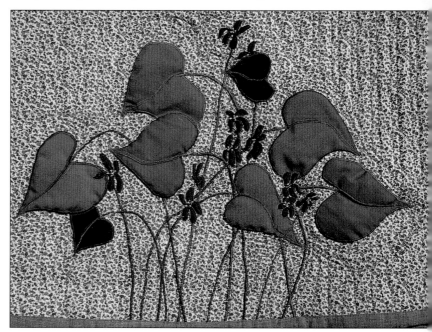

FIGURE 53. A DETAIL FROM THE REVERSIBLE SUIT SKIRT

over the ground fabric and begin with an asymmetrical shape roughly at the center of the ground.

SAMPLER 3
DISTORTED LOG CABIN BLOCK

Choose various fabrics that relate well to each other in color, value, and pattern. Strip-piece these to a ground fabric covered with a light layer of quilt batting. Begin with an asymmetrical center (no circles or curves) and continue developing this shape as you strip. Alter the strips by varying the widths and by tucking and pleating. Add lace, rickrack, or tape. Use free-motion or automatic decorative stitching and any other exciting methods you can devise to change the nature of these strips. Add at least five rounds.

Evaluate this piece in light of the traditional log cabin block. Did you find this more difficult than the chevron piecing? Compare the two results and consider how they both might be used in a piece. Does the padding enhance or detract from the final effect?

In figure 54, *Smuggler's Cave,* the entire hanging is a distorted log cabin quilt block with the added element that, beginning with the golden yellow focal point (the hidden treasure deep within the cave) the manipulated strips progress through the complete color spectrum ending with the yellow-greens at the bottom of the piece (the outside entrance to the cave). Some strips are printed, some plain. Colors are changed through overlaid layers of net, fabric crayon over print—the red-orange strip to the right of center (fig. 55), and directional change of quilted fabrics (fig. 56). The foliage at the cave entrance is a commercially printed fabric that has been changed through rearranged elements and embroidery (fig. 57). The treasure at the focal point (fig. 58), as

well as bits and pieces the smugglers dropped along the way (fig. 56) are applied beads, shisha, and buttons under tulle. Some strips

FIGURE 54. *SMUGGLER'S CAVE* INCORPORATES A DISTORTED LOG CABIN BLOCK WITH A VARIETY OF OTHER TECHNIQUES.

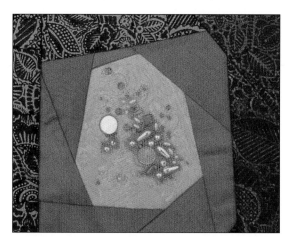

FIGURE 55. THE FOCAL POINT OF THE PIECE IS THE TREASURE TROVE, ITS "TREASURES" ENCASED IN NET.

are tucked (fig. 59) and one is pieced together from small bits of harmonizing colors and textures (fig. 60).

Many techniques are combined in this piece. The unifying element is the progression of spectrum colors and a careful use of values which accommodate the disparate fabrics involved.

FIGURE 59. TUCKED STRIPS ARE PIECED TOGETHER.

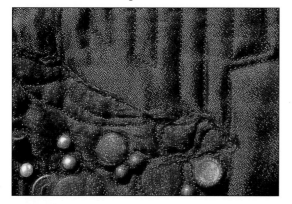

FIGURE 56. DIRECTIONAL CHANGE OF THE STITCHING ADDS INTEREST TO THE QUILTING.

FIGURE 57. YELLOW TULLE OVER CUT AND REARRANGED PRINTED FABRIC SUGGESTS SPRING GREEN.

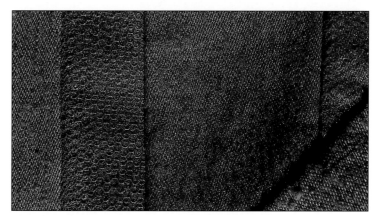

FIGURE 60. SMALL BITS OF HARMONIZING FABRICS ARE PIECED FOR ADDED TEXTURE.

CONSTRUCTING TEXTURES

Tucks, pleats, and gathers are common forms of fabric manipulation usually associated with garment construction, but they can be effectively used with embroidery.

SAMPLER 4
PLEATS, TUCKS, AND GATHERS

Use an assortment of white or pastel fabric. Experiment with at least ten different examples of tucks, pleats, and gathers. Shirring with elastic thread in the bobbin can also be used. Try pintucking with a double or triple needle (refer to your machine manual for instructions).

When you have a good supply of stitched pieces, cut them, rearrange them, and piece

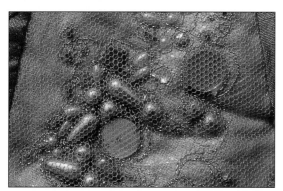

FIGURE 58. DETAIL OF TREASURES COUCHED UNDER YELLOW TULLE.

FIGURE 61. MANIPULATED FABRICS ARE PIECED TO CREATE A COLLAGE WITH TEXTURAL INTEREST.

them together with seams either on the wrong or right sides—or try both for textural changes. In general, rearrange them in such a way as to create an entirely new fabric (fig. 61).

Evaluate your results. Do you see why were you asked to use light-valued fabrics?

SAMPLER 5
TEXTURED PINTUCKING

In Sampler 4 we used the double needle for simple pintucking. Here we shall explore another way in which multiple needles combined with automatic pattern stitches can be used for changing the surface of a fabric. The type of fabric makes a difference in the results of this stitching, so a variety is encouraged for this experiment.

Remember, a multiple needle cannot swing as wide as a single one. Test the width of the needle swing by walking it through once or twice to make sure that it does not strike the edge of the foot.

MATERIALS
Work with a variety of light- to medium-weight fabrics, some printed, some plain. You will also need a double needle, a pintuck presser foot, and number 3 pearl cotton or crochet cotton of similar weight for padding.

Use a pintuck presser foot, with multiple grooves or channels on the bottom that allow

the raised tucks to pass easily through. Spacing of the double needle must correspond to the width of the grooves; consult your machine manual for detailed instructions.

With the strata configuration of bark on a tree as your inspiration, make a series of small samplers. Experiment with different width and length settings, and use the different pattern stitches available on your machine.

There are many variables here: needle width, width of needle swing (or simply a straight stitch), length of stitch, type of fabric, type of thread, colors of thread in the multiple needle as well as the bobbin, choice of pattern stitch. Newer machines that feature a backward/forward motion of the pattern offer a decided advantage in that richer, more complex textures can be created. Some machines have a small hole in the sole plate through which pearl or crochet cotton can be threaded to provide padding for one of the pintucks, resulting in yet another variable. Given the many differences in machines, plus all these variables, no one sampler will be like another, and therein lies the excitement.

SAMPLER 6
TEXTURES WITH FREE-MOTION STITCHING

Repeat the two previous experiments, but this time place the fabric in a hoop for free machining, lower the feed dogs, and work without a foot. You will find that the patterns are less distinguishable here due to the more irregular spacing of free-motion stitches, but there are advantages as well.

The swing of the needle is determined now by the width of the opening in the sole plate. Check this carefully before stitching. The stitch motion will be freer and is possible in all directions, adding further interest to the configuration of the tucks. Experiment with different combinations of the possibilities suggested above. Compare the results achieved in the two samplers, make notes on the pros and cons of both methods, and consider how both types of textured pintucking could be used to best advantage in finished pieces.

SAMPLER 7
TUCKS AND PATTERNS

Choose a variety of checked and/or plaid fabrics and handle them as you did for Sampler 4. Use some on the straight grain, some on the bias. Compare the results from this sampler with those of Sampler 2. How might this type of manipulated fabric be used with other embroidery forms?

DECONSTRUCTING, SLASHING, AND MANIPULATING

The previous samplers involved constructing new fabrics from disparate pieces of other fabrics, resulting in an entirely changed textural and color effect. In this section we shall be creating new textures and fabrics by distorting, slashing, and burning—by deconstructing rather than constructing. This should bring out that latent "Viking" element in the most timid of stitchers!

A transitional piece, *Firebird* (fig. 62), illustrates a combination of techniques involving appliqué, slashing, and fabric manipulation. In this piece two synthetic metallic fabrics, gold and red, were fused together. A piece of ordinary kitchen plastic wrap was placed between the two, then the fabric was ironed.

The components of the bird (head, body, wings, etc.) were first roughly cut from newspaper and tentatively laid out on the black ground fabric to test for scale and placement

of elements. When the composition was arranged, still subject to change, the components were cut from the fused fabric. Details of wing, feathers, and contours were developed by slashing the fabric and folding out the motifs (fig. 63). In this way both reds and golds, as well as the black negative ground, were utilized in a stylized pattern of counterbalanced design. The components were then assembled onto the black ground fabric, applied, and related by free-motion stitching.

FIGURE 62. FIREBIRD COMBINES APPLIQUÉ, SLASHING, AND MANIPULATION OF METALLIC FABRICS.

We mentioned earlier that appliqué was probably first used for strictly utilitarian purposes of reinforcing and repair-

FIGURE 63. DESIGN ELEMENTS ARE SLASHED, THEN FOLDED OUTWARD.

ing worn fabrics. Another idea from the past is the practice of slashing. Earliest forms must have originated in animal skins to allow for necessary freedom of movement. By the 16th century fashion had made the technique its own, in the form of slashed sleeves and slops (the baggy short trousers worn high on the "well-turned" legs sported by the young Henry VIII and the dashing courtiers in Elizabethan male society). Here contrasting fabrics were pulled through, puffed, and manipulated to create new textures and opulence.

A few years ago the "bloomin' vest" appeared throughout the country, available as a pattern or in kit form. Multiple layers of cotton fabrics were stitched in a grid and slashed across opposite corners. After the garment was constructed (and it had to be simple because of the bulk of the layered fabrics), the piece was put through the dryer repeatedly to fray the cut edges, assuring the desired blending of multicolored raveled edges—the ultimate in soft edge finishing. The effect was exciting, but the design left something to be desired.

Although the bulk of that garment is such that many cannot wear it well, embroiderers can do exciting things with the technique in other ways. Coats could be constructed in this way—the multi-layered fabrics contributing to the warmth of an outer garment. A panel of slashed raveling on sleeves, or around the bottom of a skirt, or worked into a mixed-media wall panel as a dramatic focal point would relate well to quilting, heavy couching, and raised stitching. The traditional grid can be distorted as shown in the drawing to create a variety of shapes and proportions of raveling to plain areas. Much can be done through selection of colors. Fabrics must be chosen carefully to assure proper raveling; pure cottons are best for this. For our first sampler we

shall work with the multi-layered sandwich of fabrics and the grid.

FIGURE 64. THE CONCENTRATION OF LINES ON A FREEFORM GRID ESTABLISHES A FOCAL POINT.

SAMPLER 8
SLASHED FABRIC

Assemble at least five lightweight cotton pieces, each approximately 12 inches (30 cm) square. Choose colors that you think work well together. As a further exercise you might choose a particular color harmony, analogous or complementary. Either would result in dramatic effects. Play with different sequences of layering. You might even cut some of the squares apart and seam them together so the sequence of colors would be different in different sections of the piece.

Position the layers to your liking, then stitch across the entire sandwich with the machine set for a regular straight stitch, dividing up the area into interesting shapes. The next step is to decide which areas will be slashed and how deeply to slash. This determines the colors that are revealed. Some slashes can go all the way to the bottom layer, others to various depths. The deeper the slash, the greater the texture and variety of colored ravels. For greatest textural effect, slashing should be done in variations of the X to allow the fabrics to turn back and ravel properly, but they do not have to be spaced symmetrically.

Geometric shapes can also be cut out, stepping the layers gradually so that a variety of colored edges are revealed. This results in a minimum amount of raveling, but it contrasts nicely with the deeper ravels and turned edges. Determine the focal point of your piece and work from there (fig. 65).

Slashing can be done with a sharp craft knife or scissors. Scissors can be controlled more easily when it comes to selecting the depth of your cut. You might even slash completely through the stack in one or two places and pull contrasting fabrics through the opening (à la Henry VIII).

The object is to play with this combination of

FIGURE 65. SLASHED AND MANIPULATED LAYERS OF FABRIC

areas, colors, and raveled textures. As you work, think how these changed surfaces might be incorporated into a larger piece. When the manipulation is completed, trim edges to notebook size and zigzag around the entire piece. Tumble in a cool dryer until a pleasing amount of raveling takes place.

Does the focal point come through strongly, or is it overpowered by the multicolored raveling? How might it be further strengthened if necessary? How might you use this technique in conjunction with other embroidery forms? How might you use this in conjunction with automatic decorative stitching?

SAMPLER 9
SLASHED FABRIC - NO RAVELING

We stressed in the previous sample the importance of using pure cotton fabrics for maximum raveling of slashed edges. Another interesting variation of this technique calls instead for synthetic double knits. For this sampler, choose a piece of polyester double knit and a piece of small-patterned polyester/cotton print that harmonize with each other.

Pin or tape the knit fabric to a cutting board. Working from a preestablished focal point out toward the edges of the fabric, make a series of cuts with sharp scissors. Make the slashes of varied sizes and angles, noticing how the edges react. Some of the edges will roll up; they can be folded back. Bias cuts react differently from those on the straight of the fabric. Experiment with different types of cuts, diagonal, X-shaped, etc.

Turn back some of the slashed edges and secure with stitching. In some cases use a presser foot and standard settings. For free machining, I suggest placing the fabric in a hoop and using either a spring shank darning

FIGURE 66. SLASHED AREAS ARE COMBINED WITH APPLIED AND UNDERLAID FABRICS.

foot or a spring needle. Some edges can simply be allowed to roll and move freely. The double knit holds its shape well, and won't ravel away.

Slash and manipulate judiciously. As you work, place the knit on top of the printed fabric and study the results. You might decide to echo some of the print colors in your stitching or to apply small areas of print to the surface of the knit. This can be an additive as well as a subtractive procedure. When you decide the slashed composition is just about finished, use enough topstitching to fasten the knit to the print. For this stitching you will probably need some added surface

stabilization—either a spring shank foot or a spring needle. To more easily see a larger area in a controlled fashion, place the two fabrics in a hoop for free machining. When the sampler is finished, trim the edges to notebook size, and zigzag around the edges.

Figures 66 and 67 show the front and back of a knit T-shirt that has been enhanced with this type of slashing. Some of the edges are stitched, some are allowed to move freely. Some of the printed fabric lies under the slashed areas, other motifs have been cut out and applied to the surface.

In figure 71, slashed areas have been used in conjunction with painted, manipulated, and burned areas. Double-knit fabric was used for this piece as well.

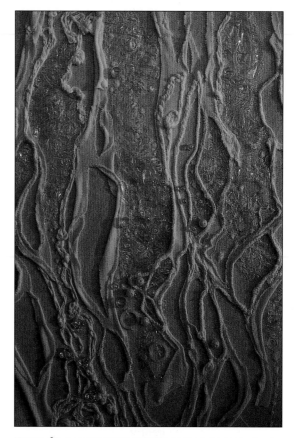

FIGURE 68. A DETAIL OF *PEAK BERNINA GLACIER*, SLASHED AND MANIPULATED KNIT FABRIC WITH BEADS

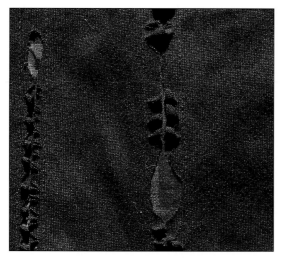

FIGURE 67. ANGLED SLASHES ARE MADE IN VERTICAL ROWS.

BURNING FABRICS

Different types of fabrics react to heat in various ways. Our first sampler involves experimenting with a variety of fabrics, and creating new textures by burning (candling). Natural fibers burn; synthetic fabrics do not. I nearly set fire to my workroom when I held a piece of cotton muslin over a candle flame, only to see it become slightly charred and smoky (lovely brown/black colors), and then suddenly burst into flame, sending flaming pieces onto my ironing surface and to the floor. I stamped out the flame on the floor and dashed to the bathroom for a wet sponge. By the time I had returned there was a six-inch circle of charring ironing pad, smoldering away and increasing in size as I watched. Needless to say, I soaked the area thoroughly, wondering how anyone could be so stupid as to allow this to happen. So my first suggestion is to place your candle on a large metal cookie sheet or similar flameproof surface before you begin the experiments. And have a wet sponge or cloth at hand.

The charred edges of cotton muslin can be interesting but they are not very stable, continuing to crumble away until much of the interesting charring is gone. I feel that the synthetic fabrics react in much more satisfying ways. Do try both, though, and decide for yourself.

Synthetic fabrics do not burn, they simply pucker, creep, and crawl when held over the flame, finally developing interesting little holes with hard, shiny, fused edges. The puckered areas form fascinating patterns in themselves, and react beautifully when sprayed lightly with gold metallic paint. The paint collects on the fused edges of the holes, providing striking contrast to the delicate gold mist on the rest of the fabric. Spraying gently across the surface accents the high spots and misses the lows,

creating even more textural interest, all of which lends itself beautifully to free-motion stitching. Caution: make a baffle of newspapers to keep spray paint from drifting.

MATERIALS

Assemble a variety of 100 percent nylon or polyester fabrics, plain and printed, light and dark (metallics and tulles are particularly effective); nylon tulle; a piece of Spandex swimsuit fabric; candle and matches; a small can of spray paint—metallic gold is a good all-purpose color; flameproof surface such as a metal baking tin; and a wet kitchen sponge.

■

SAMPLER 10

CANDLED FABRICS

Use at least ten different kinds of fabrics, including nylon tulle, and experiment with candling each piece. Hold the fabric taut over the candle flame, moving it in different directions and at different speeds, creating patterns of holes and puckers. Work with the wrong side of a printed fabric as well as the right side. Note the differences between the pile side and the smooth side of velours and velvets. As the patterns of puckers and holes develop, consider how these might be used to good advantage with stitching. Spray some with the spray paint.

Jot down notes as you experiment, recording fiber content of the fabrics if possible. Comment on the results. Slip the samples and notes into partitioned plastic pages made for mounting photographs. You can add to this sampler as you experiment with additional fabrics.

■

SAMPLER 11

A BURNED-FABRIC COMPOSITION

Choose a notebook-size piece of fabric for the ground, and select other fabrics that harmonize with it. Distress and enhance these fabrics by candling and spraying. Cut them into interesting pieces and arrange them in a pleasing composition on the ground fabric. Establish a strong focal point and pin the candled pieces in place. Choose threads for top and bobbin that echo some of the fabric colors, and place the piece in a hoop for free machining.

Use varying degrees of whipstitch, enhance the composition with straight and zigzag stitches, and at the same time secure the fabrics in place. Allow some edges to curl; fold some back to take advantage of different reverse sides. Manipulate the edges, handling them in different ways, and accent some areas with additional heavier couched threads. Does your stitching enhance and relate to the puckered pattern of the fabric?

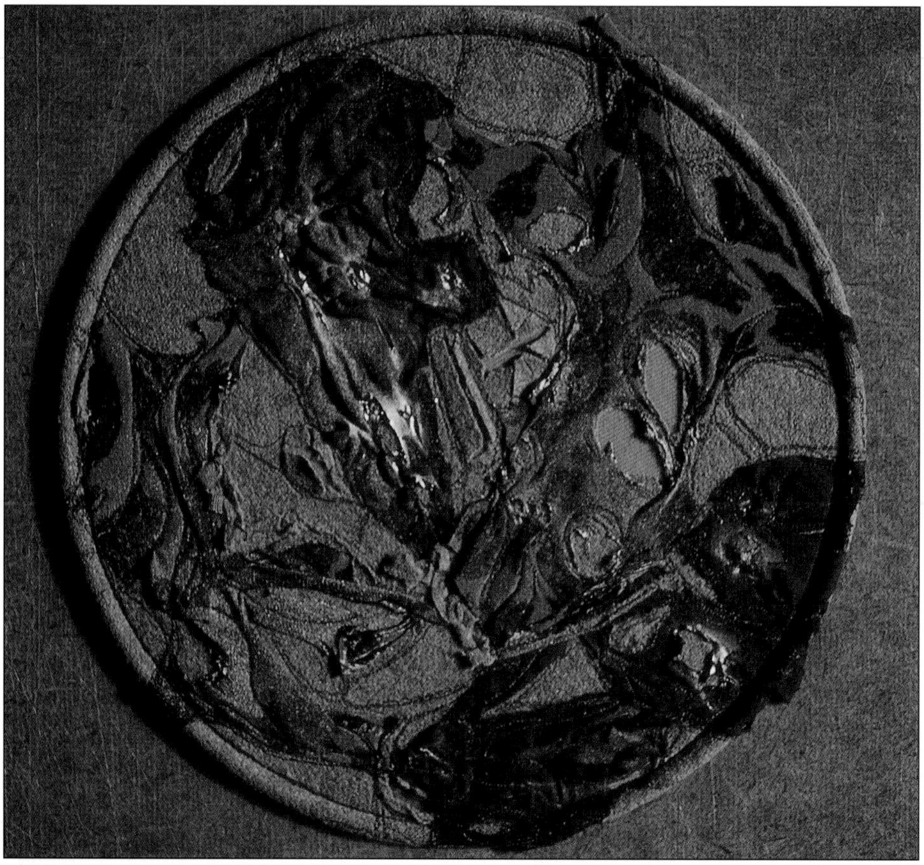

FIGURE 69. A COMPOSITION OF CANDLED, SPRAYED, AND MANIPULATED SPANDEX

SAMPLER 12
CANDLED STRETCH FABRIC

Candle and spray a piece of Spandex. Pin in place as you did in Sampler 9 and place it in a hoop for free machining. This time, as you stitch, stretch and manipulate the Spandex. You'll find it stretches much more than the knitted fabrics, causing the shapes of the holes to change as you work. Keep stretching and manipulating as you stitch. I use a double-pointed knitting needle or cuticle stick to help hold the manipulated shapes as I work—it saves wear and tear on the fingers. Leave select edges unstitched so they curl and move.

Cut narrow strips of the Spandex and couch them, twisting, turning, tying knots, and contouring as you stitch. If you are using a printed fabric or one that has a different color on the reverse, take full advantage of this difference. You'll find this an extremely mobile and versatile technique. For textural change, reframe the piece after stitching and, working from the wrong side, add some cable stitch, using number 5 pearl cotton in the bobbin.

Is the focal point of your piece strong enough to carry the weight of the couched fabrics and the cable? If not, strengthen it. How would you compare the maneuverability of the Spandex to the other knits you have used?

In figure 69 the black and blue printed fabric is Spandex.

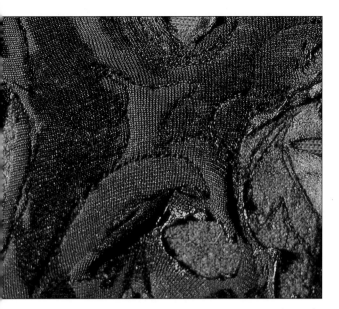

FIGURE 70. A DETAIL OF THE COMPOSITION SHOWN IN FIGURE 69

This and the plain black fabric were candled and sprayed and applied to a blue-green velour ground fabric. In figure 70, note how the Spandex was stretched, distorted, and manipulated as it was stitched.

In figure 71, the velour was slashed and manipulated, and the entire piece was mounted on top of the bright teal knit which shows through the slashing. Some of the blue-green velour was cut in narrow strips and couched. A conscious effort was made to relate all added stitching and fabrics to the puckered candled pattern of the plain black fabric.

Both the black and the iridescent fabrics in figure 72 were candled; the black was sprayed with gold. Pieces of the iridescent were cut out and applied to the black; other pieces were set under the holes of the black fabric. Note how the fused edges of the black fabric's holes pick up the gold paint. In addition, beads were strung on black, metallic thread and couched, not only echoing the nature of the fabrics, but increasing the strength of the focal point.

FIGURE 71. COUCHED STRIPS OF VELOUR. NOTE HOW THE EDGES CURL.

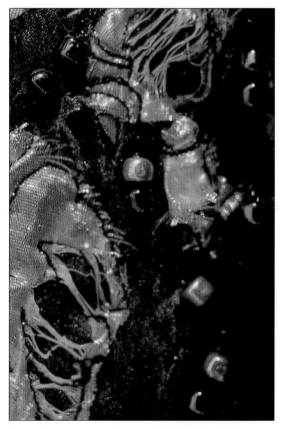

FIGURE 72. OPENWORK OF CANDLED FABRIC. STRUNG BEADS ARE COUCHED TO FORM A FOCAL POINT.

FIGURE 73. TO MAKE CUFFS FOR THE STOLE, FABRIC WAS CUT APART AND REASSEMBLED, EMBROIDERED, AND ACCENTED WITH BEADS.

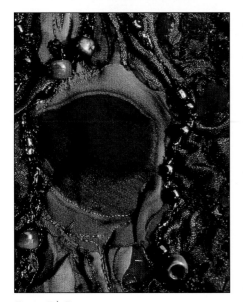

FIGURE 74. BRIGHT RED MOTIFS OF THE FABRIC ARE HIGHLIGHTED IN THE CUFFS.

to cut it up—it was beautiful as it was. Yet I wanted to use it in some way for embroidery. With just 12 inches (30.5 cm) removed from the length, I created the jeweled cuffs (fig. 74). I candled the fabric, cut it apart, then rearranged it to highlight the deep red motifs. Then it was embroidered, and beads were couched in place. The result is a simple but elegant garment that took just two yards of fabric, still showed the fabric's beautiful printed motifs, and was enriched with jewel-like, embroidered cuffs.

MANIPULATING STIFFENED FABRIC

Each time stitches are applied to the surface of fabric some degree of elevation occurs. We've achieved elevation through tucking, pleating, padding, and adding found objects to a flat surface. All these techniques heighten the concept of actual third dimension discussed in Chapter 1. An extension of this idea occurs through the use of fabric stiffeners which allow further manipulation and elevation.

For many embroiderers, the idea of stiffening fabric, basically a soft and mobile material, is offensive. And it can be. But interesting effects can be achieved through stiffening, and the ultimate challenge is to relate those stiffened areas to the soft ones in such a way that the character of the fabric is not lost. In Chapter 1 we learned the importance of contrasting hard and soft edges through stitching. Here we take the process a step further and relate hard areas to soft ones through the judicious use of stitching.

The basic principle of sculpture is to create surfaces in space so that light reacts to them in new and exciting ways. Some surfaces reflect, shadows are cast which in turn move and react to the surface upon which they fall.

As a child, I remember my grandmother wearing a woolen shawl which she kept in place by simply stitching the ends together to form an opening through which her hands were thrust—the simplest kind of cuff. I used this same principle in the stole, figure 73. I had bought only two yards of this fabric and really didn't want

Some areas are pushed back into complete shadow while others rise up to catch the light. New patterns and designs are created that can move and change as the light source changes. It is an ephemeral dimension of embroidery, and one that can be a fascinating challenge.

I find unbleached muslin easy to manipulate. Its light value reflects light and responds well to contouring. Actual stitching here will be minimal; it is important only to secure fabric pieces and serve as transition between the stiffened areas and the soft ones.

There are several stiffening agents available. Ordinary heavy laundry starch can be used if permanence is not a factor. It is a good way to play with the fabric and get the feel of the medium. For permanence I recommend commercial fabric stiffeners available in craft and fabric shops. These are usually water resistant when dry, and are unaffected by damp and humidity. They dry completely overnight, but attain a good manipulative state after about one hour.

White glue can be used, but it is a bit sticky to work with. It, like the commercial stiffeners, can be thinned slightly with water to achieve varying degrees of stiffness. Experiment with thinning to find the formula that best suits your particular project requirements.

Work on a plastic surface: a large plastic garbage bag spread on a drawing board or countertop works well and is easy to remove from the back of the dried fabric. Waxed paper also works well. Do not use foil, as it tends to stick to the stiffener buildup and often must be peeled away in bits and pieces. If a drawing board is used, it can be slipped inside the garbage bag and moved to a radiator top, or into an open gas oven where the pilot light will hasten drying. Being an impa-

tient person, I once turned the broiler on low for a few minutes to speed the drying, and got a delicately browned contour reminiscent of meringue on a pie. More lovely colors, values, and textures!

Stiffened fabrics can be bulky and unwieldy to work with on the machine, hence size is a practical consideration. I suggest you work with pieces of fabric no larger than 12 by 18 inches (30 by 46 cm) until you familiarize yourself with the techniques.

Owing to the size and the raised contours, this sample will not fit into your notebook sleeve. But this size allows for adequate fabric manipulation and yet is relatively easy to handle under the needle. Of course a great deal depends upon how high an elevation is involved. Edges 3 and 4 inches (8 and 10 cm) high are more difficult to stitch around than lower ones.

There are two basic approaches to this project, based upon a combination of cutting and manipulating fabric. Figure 75 shows a pre-stiffened piece of fabric that has simply

FIGURE 75. FABRIC MANIPULATION CREATES UNUSUAL EFFECTS WHEN THE FABRIC IS FIRST STIFFENED.

been cut with a craft knife in a geometric pattern, then folded and manipulated to form areas of light and dark. No embroidery is involved, although it could have been incorporated into the piece in various ways.

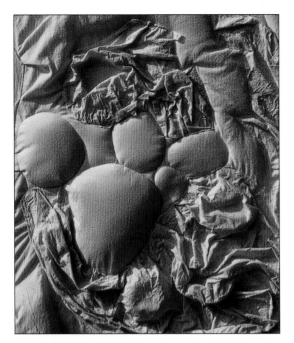

FIGURE 76. STIFFENED RAISED AREAS OF FABRIC CONTRAST WITH SOFTER ONES.

In figure 76 the fabric was soaked in stiffener, allowed to dry partially, then manipulated, shaped, and allowed to dry completely. Quilting of carefully chosen areas helped relate the stiffened raised areas to the soft ones. In this piece the fabric was manipulated before it was completely dry. Both are valid methods of working, each with completely different results.

FIGURE 77. SEMI-SOFT EDGES PROVIDE A TRANSITION BETWEEN THE SOFT CONTOURS AND CRISP RIDGES.

A great deal of tactile satisfaction is achieved by working with fabric in this way. Since the stiffener takes a number of hours to dry, the fabric remains mobile for quite some time, allowing for many revisions and changes. This process creates exciting problems in working with positive and negative areas, raised and lowered contours. Stiffened fabric edges do not ravel easily, yet raveled edges can add a good deal of interest to the piece. Figure 77 shows a semi-soft edge that serves as a reminder that we are indeed working with fabrics. This edge also provides a valid transitional element from hard area to soft.

MATERIALS

In addition to the usual supplies, this exercise requires 1 yard (1 m) of unbleached muslin, pre-washed; commercial fabric stiffener; and ½ yard (.5 m) quilt batting.

SAMPLER 13
STIFFENED FABRIC

The first step is to soak the muslin in fabric stiffener. Follow directions on the container but use the stiffener full strength. Working on a board covered with plastic or waxed paper, distort and contour the fabric. It can be folded, manipulated, scrunched up, and formed over molds such as kitchen utensils and custard cups. I usually begin roughly in the center of the piece and work out toward the edges, playing with contours as I go.

Create three or four stiffened, manipulated areas that you think would be interesting to work with, allowing some flat areas all around the raised contours.

If you have a gas oven, place the plastic on a cookie sheet and slip it or the board on an oven shelf with only the pilot light for heat to speed the drying. On a sunny day, put the board outside. A hair dryer also can be used.

Measure out two pieces of muslin for the ground fabrics, with a layer of quilt batting in between. You will probably want to make this piece larger than 8 by 11 inches (20 by 28 cm) since you'll need more space in which to work with the stiffened contours. When the stiffened pieces are completely dry, study them from all angles, cut them apart, rearrange, and re-contour as necessary to make an interesting composition of raised areas on the muslin/batting sandwich. The pieces will be stitched down and combined with free-motion quilting of the areas around them. In cutting the contours, leave some flat edges around the raised ones so the presser foot or spring needle can move around them. The edges can be irregular, manipulated, slit, or frayed to further relate them to the contours of the ground fabric. Pin them in place and secure with stitching using a presser foot and standard settings. Free machining can also be used. You will find the spring needle is a great help here since it is not possible to frame this bulky piece in a hoop.

Working roughly from the center out toward the edges, work simple machine quilting to enhance the contours of the raised areas. Use either free machining with the spring needle or darning foot, or quilting with standard settings and a regular presser foot, or a combination of the two. The intelligent embroiderer makes use of whichever methods best suit the situation. Finish the edges of the piece with zigzag stitching. The white panel (fig. 78) was worked in the above manner and mounted on a foamcore board.

If board mounting is planned, be sure to allow extra fabric on all four sides so that the excess can be brought to the wrong side and stapled or laced in place. When you mount the piece, stretch it slightly as you work. By hand, slip stitch a piece of fabric on the back for a neat finish. This can either be framed or hung as is by a cord attached to the backing.

Assess the results of your contoured piece. Does the focal point provide the necessary strong impact? Is there a pleasing transition between hard and soft areas? How does a changing light source affect the overall composition? Why were light-valued fabrics used here? What other machine techniques could be combined with this?

FIGURE 78. FABRIC CONTOURS ARE ACCENTED WITH EMBROIDERY.

You can see from the examples pictured above that very few, if any, include only one technique. Most are composites of several different methods of stitching. As you work, constantly analyze what you are doing and why certain results take place, in order to more closely relate one technique to another. As stated in the introduction, many techniques are simple. It's how they are combined and used that challenge the skill and imagination of the embroiderer.

CHAPTER 3 CUTWORK AND NEEDLE LACE

MAN HAS A LONG history of being more fascinated with viewing his world through provocative layers of sheer fabrics and patterned laces than seeing it head on. Salome used seven layers of sheers for her legendary dance; harems were traditionally hung with exotic, gossamer drapes positioned to respond to any gentle breeze (or gyration), and today one only has to notice the lingerie advertisements (especially geared for the male shopper) to realize that capital is still being made of that fascination. More to our point, the history of embroidery provides vivid and varied evidence that suggestion is superior to revelation, subtlety rather than the obvious, understated elegance rather than overwhelming richness. Most obvious manifestations of this principle can be seen in the variety of lace, cutwork, and shadow work that remains. Fortunes have been made and lost in the manufacture of lace and speculation on its value. Although its monetary value as a product varies with the whims of fashion, the aesthetic appreciation of it remains unchanged.

There are two basic forms of lace. Bobbin lace and needle lace (needlepoint) involve creating new fabrics through looping, knotting, and combining threads controlled by either bobbins or needles. The lace threads become the entire fabric. Cutwork—Richelieu, Renaissance, reticella—is formed through a working relationship between embroidery and fabric that has been cut and manipulated to respond to the stitching.

Traditionally, lace has been stiffened by some means in order to reveal the intricate patterns of its designs. Extreme examples of this can be seen in 16th-century portraits of most European monarchs, particularly Elizabeth I

of England, and in those of wealthy church and secular officials of the time. Clearly, lace had become a status symbol. Later fashion trends set a bunch of lace at throat and wrists, but now much of the actual pattern became elegant texture rather than recognizable design because stiffening was relaxed.

There is still something to be said for the fascination of the suggested, but today our methods and sensibilities dictate that for that casual touch of lace at throat and wrist, or wherever, machine-made yardage, readily available and quite inexpensive, usually serves. Intricate handmade lace is still admired and treasured, usually in our museums or handed down as cherished family heirlooms from one generation to the next. lt is either stiffly starched or mounted in some way that the pattern is clear and distinct, or it is stretched on a frame or attached to a ground fabric. This latter method, however, negates one characteristic of lace: the effect of light coming through the openings of its fabric.

In machine embroidery, where a taut surface is absolutely necessary for satisfactory results, stabilization is particularly important when working with open areas of lace. When I began working with machine-stitched lace, one carefully stretched fabric tightly in a hoop, delineated an area for lace or cutwork, stitched several rows of straight stitching around that area, cut it out, and worked a pattern of lace in the air, across the open space. To say the least, this method required a good deal of patience and skill to accomplish—and resulted in many frustrated stitchers. This is still a valid method for machine-made lace. In recent years, however, new products have been introduced that add vastly to the possibilities of machined cutwork and lace.

When I studied in England, vanishing muslin was used by most English machine embroiderers. Stitching was done on this muslin-like fabric, which was then removed with a hot iron to leave only the stitching. This worked fairly well with English direct current irons, but American irons, using alternating current, were not hot enough to disintegrate the vanishing muslin. Fortunately, new materials have solved the problem.

STABILIZERS

There are currently two kinds of commercially made disintegrating stabilizer available for machine embroidery. One is a water-soluble film, a material originally developed for hospital use as laundry bags in contagion wards. It is sold under various trade names. It is inexpensive, transparent, strong, slightly stretchy, and disintegrates in water. It can be framed in a hoop like fabric or used in conjunction with fabric for many different stabilization needs. It is available packaged or by the yard from craft shops, fabric shops, embroidery mailorder outlets, and sewing machine shops. It does require the use of a hoop, and presupposes that the materials used will not be damaged by water.

The water-soluble stabilizer is a great boon to machine embroiderers. It can be used in a variety of ways. A design can be drawn or traced on it, the film then placed on the fabric and framed in a hoop, and stitching worked through both layers. To draw the design, use a waterproof pen made for this purpose to make sure the marks will wash away completely. Do not use a water-based pen as it can bleed into your fabric. Permanent markers are equally unacceptable.

FIGURE 79. *DUSTIN'S QUILT* WAS MADE USING WATER-SOLUBLE STABILIZER TO HOLD PIECES OF THE FABRIC COLLAGE IN PLACE FOR STITCHING.

The film can also be used on top of a fabric collage to hold all the bits and pieces in place until stitching is completed. A few pins and the pressure of the hoop makes this possible. *Dustin's Quilt* (fig. 79), a four-seasons, tree of life quilt made for our second grandchild, was constructed by this method.

After the embroidery is finished, spray the piece with water, or dip it. The film disappears along with any paint-drawn lines.

The film also serves as stabilizer. It reduces the danger of puckering when closely spaced stitching is used on lightweight fabric, and it simplifies work with stretch fabrics. Figure 80 shows an embroidered peacock feather worked directly on a purchased cotton/polyester knit sweatshirt. The design was drawn on the film, pinned in position on the shirt and framed up. Stitching was done directly on the design through the film, which was then dissolved away. The knit fabric didn't stretch or pucker.

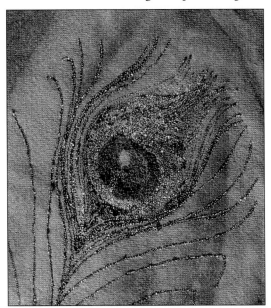

FIGURE 80. WATER-SOLUBLE FILM WAS USED TO STABILIZE KNIT FABRIC FOR STITCHING.

As you investigate this film further, you'll discover many more uses for it. We'll be working with it in this chapter and Chapter 5 in a variety of ways.

The second type of stabilizer disintegrates with heat. It can be ironed away, or the piece can be placed in a regular oven set at 300 degrees. It also can be removed with a heat gun—the kind sold for burning paint from wood. Care must be exerted to find the proper distance from the embroidery, since there is no heat control on most guns. Experiment with a sample before using the heat gun on a finished piece.

There are a number of these heat-reactive stabilizers available. One kind is much like the English vanishing muslin, and works best framed in a hoop. Another product is a heavier, scrim-like fabric, stiff enough to allow stitching with the bare needle and without a hoop—a great advantage in many cases.

Both these, unlike the water-soluble film, will leave residue in the form of a charred crumble of fabric, or a brittle web of blackened scrim. The residue can be removed by breaking it away carefully and gently brushing the embroidered area with a small, stiff brush. Special care must be taken to avoid damaging fragile stitching. These stabilizers are more expensive than the water-soluble film, and, depending upon the concentration of stitches used, it is more difficult to remove the residue.

Another disadvantage of the scrim-type stabilizer is that heat used to remove the material will darken some threads, particularly the lighter valued hues and whites. I've even had crochet cotton disintegrate in the oven.

Experiment with both types of stabilizer. Become familiar with their characteristics, then decide which suits the needs of your particular piece.

A word of caution: I have found that the heat-reactive stabilizers create strong chemical fumes and must be used only sparingly and in a well-ventilated room. Try not to inhale those fumes. If you suffer from severe inhalant allergies, do not use this stabilizer; use the water-solubles exclusively.

DESIGNING OPENWORK

Any good design should have a pleasing relationship between the positive, or stitched, areas and the negative, or unstitched, ones. Never is this more apparent than when working with lace. The major impact of the design involves open space. To achieve this impact, we shall distort fabric, open up areas, and turn empty space into interesting areas formed by stitching.

For our purpose there are two major categories of lace and openwork. The first one we shall address is cutwork, which combines patterns of stitched threads combined with open areas of fabrics. The second type, explored later in the chapter, involves patterns of stitches worked in the air and involves no fabric but that created by the threads of the stitching.

Materials
In addition to basic tools and supplies, you will need the following materials for the exercises in this section: 3 yards (2.75 m) Battenberg lace tape; two 15-inch (38-cm) squares of organdy or some other sheer, firm fabric; a coarse, loosely woven fabric such as burlap or remnant of drapery fabric. You'll also need 1 yard (1 m) of nylon tulle. A rotary cutter and mat are handy but not absolutely necessary. You will also need five or six 9- or 10-inch (23- or 25.5-cm) metal rings; one 5-inch (12.5-cm) ring, and two 2- or 3-inch (5- or 7.5-cm) rings of the type used for macramé. You will need 2 yards (1.85 m) of water-soluble film; 1 yard (1 m) of heat-reactive scrim; tacky glue; a white paint marking pen to use on the film. Read the labels carefully; some pens are made for just this purpose, but others are simply labeled "white paint, fine line."

Needle Lace Combined with Fabric

Cutwork involves carefully selected areas of fabric that are cut out. The remaining edges are finished in a variety of ways. It is these open areas, combined with the remaining fabric, that form the design pattern of the piece. In simplest terms, fabric and space, enhanced with stitching, create a pattern of lace by combining positive and negative areas. This usually happens on a simple and relatively large scale.

Sampler 1
Cutwork

For this exercise we'll use a square of organdy and a square of water-soluble film. Plan a design that will fill the inner ring of the hoop, creating open spaces of different sizes and shapes. Observe the characteristics of a good composition, such as a strong focal point and a pleasing relationship between positive and negative areas. The strength of your composition depends a great deal upon the size and placement of these open spaces. Draw the design on the film with a white paint marking pen.

Position the film design on the *reverse* side of the organdy, and frame it in the hoop for free-motion stitching. With a spring needle, straight stitch at least three closely spaced rows around each space to be cut away. The stitching not only reinforces the edges of the areas to be cut out, but marks these areas on the fabric.

To cut out the areas, use very sharp scissors and cut *only through the fabric, not through the film.* Cut with the palm of your hand *upward* (downward if you are left-handed) to avoid cutting the stay stitching. If you make a miscut and remove some of the film, don't worry. Simply pin another piece of film under the damaged area and continue.

Now is the time to make decisions. Edges around the open spaces should be finished (remember the hard and soft edges discussed in Chapter 1?), and stitching should be related to the areas of open space. In figure 81, cutwork is combined with double-needle stitching (both free and with presser foot), simple straight stitching, and stitching with hemstitch needle. On natural cotton organdy this needle leaves an interesting pattern of little holes. Decide what stitching will best relate to your pattern of cutwork, and complete the embroidery.

Crop the piece if necessary to fit your notebook page, and finish the edges. Immerse the piece in water to remove the film and allow to dry. You will discover that if a small amount of stabilizer water remains in the fabric, some stiffness occurs. This can be beneficial in some fabrics, such as organdy. If you remove all the stabilizer, spray starch and a gentle touch-up with the iron will serve as well. What ideas do you have for using this technique in other types of embroidery?

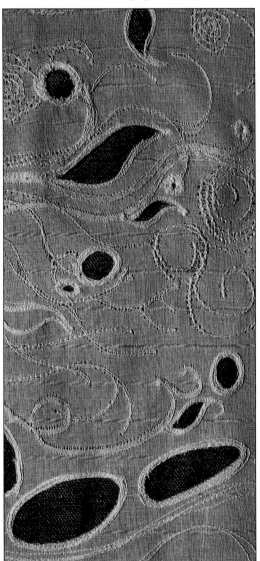

FIGURE 81. A DOUBLE NEEDLE WAS USED TO STITCH THIS CUT-WORK PIECE.

CUTWORK COMBINED WITH LACE FILLING

Using the second piece of organdy, plan areas of cutwork as for Sampler 1, and frame for free machining. This time, in conjunction with a variety of finished edges, fill the open spaces with interesting patterns of needle-stitched lace. Straight stitch across the openings in such a way that patterns of threads are built up to form the lace. Make sure the threads are firmly anchored, not only at the edges of the opening, but by stitching across threads within the open area so that when the stabilizer is removed, the thread pattern will retain its shape (see fig. 94).

Some zigzag can be worked on top of the straight stitching, to add heavier texture in contrast to the straight stitched threads. Small blobs can also be worked on these spanning threads for a slightly beaded effect. Experiment with different patterns of lace filling, and different decorative edges for finishing the cut-out areas as shown in the drawing.

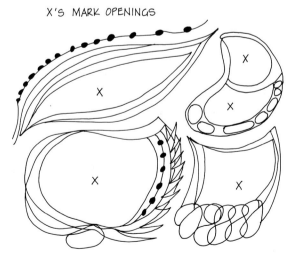

FIGURE 82. IN CUTWORK, EDGE FINISHES CAN SUPPLY ADDITIONAL TEXTURE.

Combine with hemstitching or multiple needle pintucking on the fabric areas if you wish.

■

LACE MADE FROM FABRIC

In the next samplers we will work with completely different fabrics, and with quite different results. In the preceding exercises we cut out areas of the fabric, filled the resulting openings with patterns of stitching, and related these areas to the plain fabric with hemstitching and/or pintucking. Now we will be turning the actual fabric into lace by two new methods. One involves manipulating the warp and weft threads of the fabric; the other involves slashing the fabric. Your next sampler addresses the first method—manipulation of warp and weft.

■

SAMPLER 3

WARP AND WEFT MANIPULATION

Frame a piece of loosely woven, coarse fabric. Cut a few warp and weft threads at approximately the center of the piece. Start pulling out these threads in both directions, working from the center out toward the edges. At first, remove threads from an area no more than 4 inches (10 cm) square. A large darning needle or a double-pointed knitting needle works well for this process, and you might find it easier if the fabric is framed in a hoop.

Don't pull out the raveled threads entirely; allow them to dangle from the fabric for the moment. Instead of removing all the threads, allow some to remain for stitching. This is a time-consuming job, but well worth the effort. More can be removed as you progress.

It is important to frame the fabric firmly in the hoop since the open spaces will relax the surface tension necessary for free-motion

stitching. Use a spring needle to further stabilize your fabric. A darning foot would most likely be too bulky, catching in loose threads and causing general irritation.

Lace is formed by zigzag stitching on the remaining warp and weft threads, clumping them together into interesting patterns of positive and negative space (fig. 83). I usually use the widest needle swing for this clumping. Support the surface firmly with your fingers and learn to move freely in all directions. You can add a layer of film under the fabric for further stabilization, but I usually prefer to work only with the fabric and threads. The threads seem freer to move and clump without the film. Try both techniques, though, to see which works best for you.

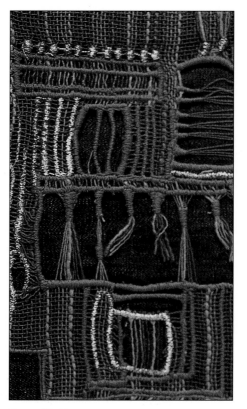

FIGURE 83. MANIPULATED WARP AND WEFT LACE

You'll find you can stitch over empty space or simply secure the thread in one area and, with presser foot raised, extend the threads to the next edge, and secure the other end. Use only a straight stitch. This and the extended threads can be overstitched with zigzag if you choose, but a web of straight stitch or spanning thread is necessary for a foundation. Zigzag done without this foundation forms an interesting chenille-like effect, but it is difficult to control unless the lace is later

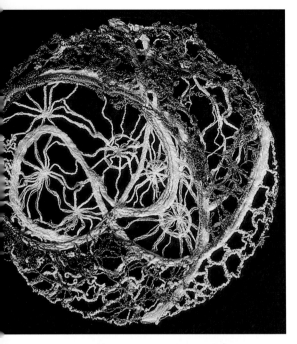

FIGURE 84. ZIGZAG STITCH WORKED WITHOUT FOUNDATION STITCHING PRODUCES A CHENILLE-LIKE TEXTURE.

mounted on another fabric. In this case, the chenille can be manipulated and couched (fig. 84).

Keep the stitching going steadily across the opening and support the edges firmly with your fingers. If you pause, the bobbin thread will often whip up and break. Once you get the feel of the techniques, you'll find all kinds of interesting areas can be manipulated and opened up.

Concentrate on variety in size and shape of open areas, and interesting concentrations of stitching. Remove more warp and weft threads as you go, until the entire piece is worked as lace. Those loose threads can be worked back into the piece, stitched over, and used as additional texture and support for edges of the openwork (fig. 85).

The finished area of lace should be approximately the size of your notebook page. Finish

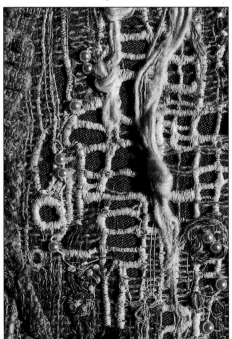

FIGURE 85. WARP AND WEFT MANIPULATION, WITH LOOSE THREADS KNOTTED AND STITCHED INTO THE PIECE

the edges and slip into a notebook sleeve along with your comments.

■

HEAVIER TEXTURED LACE

Work another piece using the same procedure as for Sampler 3. This time add heavier yarn as you form the lace. Tie some knots and relate the stitching to those knots. String beads on some threads, separating the beads enough to anchor the intervening threads with stitching, and relate them to the textures of the knots, thus enhancing the variety and texture of your lace (fig. 86). Trim and finish the edges. Figure 87 shows a detail of a caftan that was worked by this method.

■

SLASHED FABRIC LACE

In the previous chapter slashing was used as a form of fabric manipulation. Here we'll turn it into lace.

FIGURE 86. BEADS HAVE BEEN ADDED TO A HEAVIER TEXTURED LACE.

FIGURE 87. NEEDLE LACE USED ON THE YOKE OF A CAFTAN

Frame up a piece of muslin or percale (we want a firmer, more closely woven fabric for this sampler). With very sharp scissors or a rotary cutter, make two or three slashes in the fabric, each not more than 2 or 3 inches (5 to 7.5 cm) long. Each slash reduces the surface tension of the fabric, and this can cause problems. As you gain more experience with this technique, you will learn just how much slashing at one time, and in what position, will best suit your type of fabric and needs.

Use a wide zigzag to carefully stitch around the slashed openings, allowing the fabric to move and clump under the needle. Depending upon how far apart the slashes are, there may be small amounts of fabric left, or none at all. Experiment with different spacing of slashes and directional change—different results occur with the grain or on the bias. Take advantage of these differences. Try to taper the stitching at the top and bottom

of the slash and work in other embroidery stitches as you go, relating the open space to the closed. I find thick and thin lines and blobs work well. Figure 88 shows this technique combined with woven strips of fabric.

If you have trouble stabilizing the edges of the slashes, use a pencil with the point broken off, or a cuticle stick to hold the edges in place as you stitch. Cut thin strips of the fabric and work them in as additional texture, using them as you would heavy yarn. Knot, twist, and manipulate them as you stitch. Work some of the areas with a piece of stabilizing film pinned behind the fabric and see which method you find more successful. Do you find this technique more, or less, interesting than the method used for Samplers 3 and 4? Why?

SAMPLER 6
COLLAGE UNDER TULLE

Place a piece of muslin or percale on the outer ring of the hoop. Arrange beads, buttons, bits of fabrics and threads, knotted cords, and other found objects into an interesting composition. When you are satisfied with the arrangement, carefully cover the entire fabric

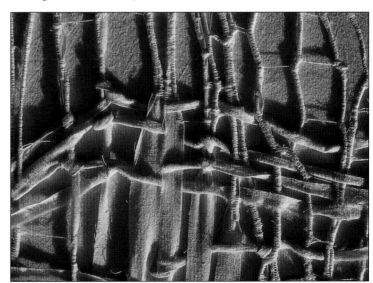

FIGURE 88. FABRIC STRIPS ARE WOVEN IN TO SLASHED LACE.

FIGURE 89. SLASHED LACE IS USED TO SUGGEST GARDEN FLOWERS AND FOLIAGE.

with a piece of tulle. Secure the found objects with long pins and frame carefully and tightly with the inside hoop.

Begin enhancing the composition with free machining, couching, or whatever techniques you choose. At intervals, slash clusters of slits in the fabric and work the resultant fabric strips as needle lace. Continue to slash and stitch, relating the pattern of negatives to the added elements as well as to any machine embroidery. Make the stay stitching around the found objects aesthetically pleasing as well as functional. Experiment with different sizes and directions of slash. Vary the concentration of the holes. Try to relate the areas of lace to the rest of the piece, forming them as an organic element of the whole (fig. 89).

Make notes on the results of your work, including the joys and problems you encountered. Add them to your notebook along with the sampler.

SAMPLER 7
MOUNTING ON A RING

In working with any open areas, there is always the problem of the open places collapsing and spoiling the patterns created by the spaces. For this reason, most lace is slightly stiffened or supported in some way for maximum appreciation of the design. One easy method of supporting your lace pattern is to mount the fabric on a metal ring of the type available in craft centers for use with macramé. They are available in diameters ranging from approximately 2 to 24 inches (5 to 61 cm). A ring supports the fabric, and provides a frame as well. I have used this method to mount and frame a number of my pieces. The rings are lightweight, sturdy, inexpensive, and easily transported. Using combinations of any/all of the techniques explored in the previous three exercises, create a piece of lace to be mounted on a 9- or 10-inch (23- to 25.5-cm) metal ring.

Work with a piece of fabric at least 3 inches (7.5 cm) larger all around than your finished size. You'll need excess to frame the piece in your hoop for working and later for mounting on the ring. In addition, the extra fabric allows for some maneuverability in placing the embroidery in a position on the ring which best enhances the composition. Work the stitches at least 2 inches (5 cm) beyond the perimeter of the ring so you can take advantage of this maneuverability.

After the embroidery is completed, reset the machine for standard sewing. Stitch two closely spaced rows of long basting stitches, stitching 2 inches (5 cm) beyond the outer rim of the embroidery. Don't lock the beginning and ending of these rows. Pull up on the threads to gather, shaping the fabric gently around the metal ring mobcap fashion. Pull the threads as tightly as possible, distributing gathers evenly, and tie threads securely.

For a large piece, for a 24-inch (61-cm) ring, for example, instead of using gathering stitches, zigzag carefully over a heavier cord or strong string. Use a wide-grooved foot and long stitch setting. Take care not to catch the cord in the stitching.

Position the embroidery on the ring to best enhance the composition. Move it right, left, up, or down, until you are satisfied. Working on the right side, firmly secure the fabric to the ring by placing long quilter's pins at right angles to the ring. Pin top and bottom, left and right; then work between these pins, placing the pins about 1 inch (2.5 cm) apart, and stretching the fabric firmly as you go. Take care not to distort the pattern of lace or bend the ring.

With a zipper foot and thread to match the fabric, work two rows of short straight stitch on the right side, stitching as closely as possible to the inside rim of the ring. Sew around again with a short, very narrow zigzag, testing the setting by walking the machine through the first stitch to make sure the needle doesn't hit the foot or the ring.

On the back of the piece, pull the excess fabric firmly away from the ring and trim it carefully close to the stitching. Use very sharp scissors (dressmaker's shears work better than small embroidery scissors), and cut with the palm of your hand upward (downward if you are left handed). Pull the excess fabric firmly away from the stitching next to the ring, and carefully cut away the excess fabric close to the stitching. The result is a firm, neatly stretched fabric, and also allows you to do additional stitching on the piece, if you feel the need, without using a hoop. On large circles it won't be possible to reach the center of the circle, but quite a bit of the outer edge can still be worked.

To hang your piece, cut heavy thread or cord approximately 5 inches (12.5 cm) longer than the span of your ring. The span should be measured 3 to 4 inches (7.5 to 10 cm) below the top center of the ring. Tie a heavy knot approximately 1 inch (2.5 cm) from one end of the cord. Position this knot touching the inside of the ring on the reverse of the piece. Very carefully stitch on the right side close to the ring, securing the knot in position. Stretch the cord across to the opposite side. Tie a heavy knot in the proper position and stitch in place. Touch the underside of each knot with a small dot of tacky glue and allow it to dry.

Trim off excess at the ends of the cord. Sign your piece, and it is ready to hang and be enjoyed.

If your piece is primarily lace, the cord will obviously show. Lace circles can be hung through a strategically placed opening in the lace, supported by the metal ring. Since the piece is light in weight, a tiny nail will support it nicely and will not be obvious.

HEAT-REACTIVE STABILIZERS

As mentioned earlier, there is a stabilizer available that is similar to English vanishing muslin, but adapted to the temperatures of American irons. It can be used much like the water soluble film, but is removed by heat rather than water. A hoop should be used with this stabilizer. The scrim-type stabilizer has enough body to make the hoop unnecessary; however, I have found that working with the scrim-type stabilizer presents some problems (see page 52) that should be investigated before you begin to stitch.

MATERIALS
You will need, in addition to the supplies listed on page 53: A variety of fabrics of different fiber contents, colors, and weaves, including some nylon tulle; 1 yard (1 m) scrim-type heat-reactive stabilizer; found

objects such as beads, plastic (berry box mesh, six-pack rings, etc.); a partitioned plastic notebook sleeve like that used for displaying photographs.

■

SAMPLER 8

EXPERIMENTING WITH HEAT-REACTIVE STABILIZER

In this excercise you will actually be making a number of samplers. The object of this experiment is to test different fabrics and threads to see how they react to the heat of an iron and an oven. Cut strips and small pieces of the variety fabrics to be used in conjunction with different threads. Pin these fabric bits to a 16-inch (40.5 cm) square of heat-sensitive scrim to create at least 10 very small samplers. Allow space within each sampler that can later be filled with needle lace.

Join and enhance the fabrics within each small square with a variety of threads—pearl cotton, rayon, metallics, cotton/polyester, silk—filling the spaces with patterns of needle lace. Add some beads, bits of plastic, or polymer clay objects if you wish. Experiment with different stitch techniques, such as whip, cable, and couching. Make sure that all threads are securely attached in such a way that when the scrim is removed, the open areas are adequately supported. As you work, note the fiber content of both fabric and threads, and the types of stitching done. Cut the scrim in half, with at least five stitched samples on each half.

Place one set of samples on a sheet of typing paper, then on a metal cookie tin; heat it in a 300-degree oven for about 15 minutes. Since ovens vary to a certain extent, check periodically. Remove when the scrim becomes dark and charred looking. It should be very brittle; if it is not, allow it to bake longer. Break and

crumble the excess scrim away, and brush out the remaining bits with an old toothbrush.

Note the appearance of the different threads and fabrics. Have changes occurred with the heating? What happens to the synthetic fabrics? The plastics? The beads? Attach these notes to the appropriate sample and slip each one into a section of the plastic sleeve.

Heat the other half of the samples with the iron. Place them between two layers of typing paper and iron with a moderately hot, dry iron. Check to see at what point the scrim begins to crumble and char, and remove the residue as above. Observe the results, and make notes to keep with the samples.

■

One of my experiments with this material produced fascinating results. I had made a fabric collage of strips of nylon and polyester fabrics, and enhanced them with a combination of metallic, cotton/polyester, and rayon threads, all worked on a piece of heat-reactive scrim. Beads were strung on some of the threads, and I manipulated the strips of fabric as I stitched. The result was an interesting, heavily textured composition of lace. I put it in the oven at 300 degrees for 15 minutes and upon checking it found not much had happened. This might have been the result of the heavy buildup of fabrics and threads. I turned up the oven to 350 and left it in to bake a bit longer. Suddenly the smoke alarm went off, and a little puff of smoke emerged when I opened the oven door. My lovely lace composition had changed! The threads and beads seemed unaffected by the higher heat, but the synthetic fabrics had melted and fused to the pattern of threads. Although the fabric colors were lost, the remaining threads, coated with the melted fabric, took on a wonderful iridescent, slightly metallic appearance. There had also been some contraction and stiffening, so that the center of the piece was slightly raised above the surface of the edges.

When the thing cooled off I mounted it on a contrasting piece of fabric that had been distressed by burning, then on a piece of black tulle. The three-layered piece was then mounted on a ring. Due to the fused fabrics and the three layers, the whole piece has a wonderful three-dimensional effect and an unusually subtle richness that I've been able to achieve in no other way (fig. 90).

I tell this to illustrate the importance of experimenting and of taking notes on what you do and what results occur. With the variety of fabrics and threads available today, with different percentages of fiber contents, and a variety of weaves, it is almost impossible to predict exact results. This can be half the fun. Take the time to play with different materials, and keep a record of what happens. And always think in terms of using what you've discovered in some future piece of embroidery.

FIGURE 90. THIS FUSED FABRIC LACE WAS AN ACCIDENT—WITH HAPPY RESULTS!

■

SAMPLER 9
A COLLAGE WITH HEAT-REACTIVE SCRIM

Choose some of the samples you like best from the previous exercise (or better still, make some new ones) and combine those pieces in a fabric collage. Pin the materials to a square of heat-sensitive scrim. Using free machining without a hoop, develop patterns of lace between the fabrics, manipulating and enhancing the fabric pieces as you work. Make a special effort to relate the patterns of lace to the rest of the embroidery. When the stitching is completed, remove the scrim by either ironing or heating in the oven. Put the piece into your

notebook as is, or mount it first on a harmonizing ground fabric.

■

SAMPLER 10
FUSED FABRICS

Make a similar composition using 100 percent nylon fabrics, including some metallics. Combine these with patterns of lace in variety threads, and some beads if you choose. Set the oven at approximately 350 degrees and experiment with the fabric fusion described above. Keep watch over the experiment while it is in the oven. Take notes and describe your results. How does this piece differ from the previous samplers?

■

New and different kinds of stabilizers are becoming available every year. The entire field of fabrics, threads, and accessories is a rapidly changing one, and the active machine embroiderer certainly must keep up with new products. If you have some idea of the effects you wish to achieve, keep reading, exploring, and testing these products to see what they will do for you. And don't hesitate to push them beyond what the manufacturer intends them to do.

BATTENBERG LACE

When I was small my mother made all my dresses—beautifully smocked ones, and some with yokes made of fagoting. For the fagoting she basted rows of bias tape to a piece of brown paper, then worked hand stitching (usually a form of cretan stitch or herringbone) between those rows. The piece was then removed from the paper, revealing a pattern of lace formed by the tape and stitches. Of course, not appreciating the unique and beautiful handmade quality of them, I always secretly longed for "store-bought" ones. I've not seen fagoting used very much since then, but in recent years there has been a revival of Battenberg lace, which is closely akin to fagoting. In Battenberg lace, a special flexible, lace-like tape is basted to paper in prescribed patterns or design motifs. Filling stitches are then worked from one edge of the tape to another to create another form of lace that combines fabric tape and embroidery. Until the advent of water-soluble stabilizers, this type of lace could not be made on the machine.

Ashes of Roses, figure 91, is an example using machine-made Battenberg lace. A double layer of water-soluble stabilizer is used as a ground, the design drawn on the stabilizer with a white paint pen. Battenberg tape is then pinned to the design.

Fine gathering threads are woven into both edges of the Battenberg tape. These can be gently drawn up, allowing the tape to be contoured to form curves, both to the right and the left, depending upon which basting thread is drawn. Raw ends of the tape are carefully turned under, to be secured later with stitching. The piece is framed up in a hoop, and filling stitches are worked between the lines of tape, not only to secure the tape but to enhance the design. The very nature of the materials, strips of tape with filling stitches, dictates a quite simple, stylized design.

The illustrated piece was mounted on a ring after the stitching was finished, then the stabilizer was dissolved. *Voilà*, a modern machine-embroidered piece of Battenberg lace!

Battenberg lace actually combines fabric and embroidery, as explored earlier in this chapter. Since mounting this type of lace is a bit more complex, I chose to include it here simply because you have by now had some experience with this type of finishing.

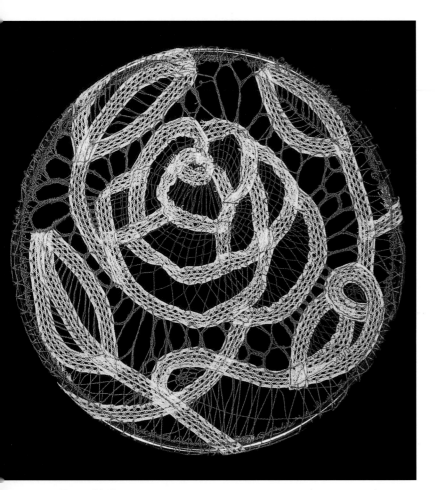

FIGURE 91. BATTENBERG LACE, EMBROIDERED BY MACHINE

SAMPLER 11
BATTENBERG LACE

On layout or tracing paper, plan and draw a design for Battenberg lace to fit a 9-inch (23-cm) metal ring. Keep the design simple, with strong linear elements that can be formed with tape and connected with patterns of lace. Concentrate on an interesting variety of spaces between those lines. Your design can be either representational (like the rose design in figure 91) or entirely abstract. Allow some of the lines to extend at least to the edge of the ring, with some extending beyond it. When the design pleases you, strengthen the lines with a black felt pen.

Place this pattern under a double layer of water-soluble stabilizer, at least 14 inches (36 cm) square and trace the design onto the film with a white paint pen. Carefully frame the piece in a 10-inch (25.5-cm) hoop. Working in a hoop slightly larger than the finished size of the piece allows elements to be extended beyond the perimeter of the design, and the piece will not have to be repositioned during stitching.

Pin strips of Battenberg tape to the stabilizer to delineate the design lines of the pattern. At curves, gently draw up the gathering thread on the appropriate edge of the tape to contour it to the design. Turn under raw ends of tape where joins occur, and plan to secure these joins as you stitch. Tighten the film in the hoop if necessary before stitching.

Fill the intervening spaces between the lines of tape with a variety of needle lace fillings. Remember, when the stabilizer is removed, only the lace fillings will support the tape and keep those elements from collapsing. Be sure to secure all stitching firmly to the edges of the tape.

Interesting patterns of fillings, concentration

of stitches, and direction of stitches are very important in this type of lace. In figure 91 the positive areas (the rose, bud, and leaf motifs) were filled with more closely spaced patterns of lace. The negative areas were filled with heavier stitching, but it was worked farther apart (fig. 92). This is one device for indicating the important difference between positive and negative elements of the design. Extend unsupported lace fillings a bit beyond the perimeter of the ring to assure their being caught into the lines of mounting stitching.

Mounting on the ring is a bit more difficult in this case since there is very little actual fabric involved. Care

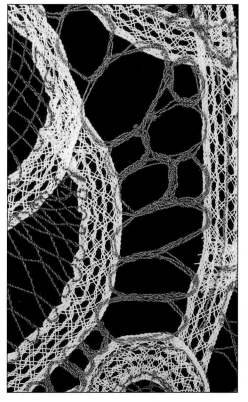

FIGURE 92. A VARIETY OF LACE FILLINGS CAN BE USED WITH THE BATTENBERG TAPE.

must be taken not to tear the film; however, another layer of film can be added at this point for reinforcement. Carefully remove the stitched film from the hoop, and stitch around the perimeter of the circle as described on page 58. Pin the film and tape ends carefully onto the ring, pulling gently to make the piece taut and firm. Finish by stitching three times around the outside edge of the embroidery as described for Sampler 7, page 58. At the same time, firm up the tension of the lace. Assess your work critically. If there are relaxed threads remaining, they can still be restitched and repaired at this point. Dangling or relaxed threads around the perimeter can be picked up with the needle and stretched and walked over the rim of the ring. Offending areas of lace can be cut out, backed with more film, and restitched; a firm ring mount serves the purpose of a hoop. This is a more difficult form of mounting than some, but happily, repairs are easy and are possible at almost any stage of the process. After all threads are taut and secured, dip the ring in water, blot with a towel, and allow to dry. What other ways can you think of to mount and use this type of lace?

AIRBORNE NEEDLE LACE

The previous exercises all involved lace combined with some form of fabric—fabric used as a co-element along with the stitching threads, fabric as a ground for the composition, or strips of fabric used in place of heavy threads. In the next exercises we shall create lace with only the stitching threads. There are several ways in which to do this lace. It can be worked entirely on water-soluble stabilizer, it can be stiffened with fabric stiffener and unmounted (fig. 93), or it can be made without stiffening, mounted on a garment or some other piece of fabric and combined with other types of embroidery.

Another approach is to work on a layer of water-soluble film plus a layer of white or pastel tulle. These two layers are mounted on a metal ring and the tulle is cut away before the lace is begun. Here the mounting ring takes the place of the hoop. The film is dissolved after the lace is worked, leaving over the ring only a firm edge of tulle into which the lace stitching has been attached. Slack threads can be taken up by stretching and walking them over the rim (fig. 94). The vanishing muslin type of stabilizer can also be used, but since it is handled like the water-soluble film, except that it is removed with a hot iron instead of

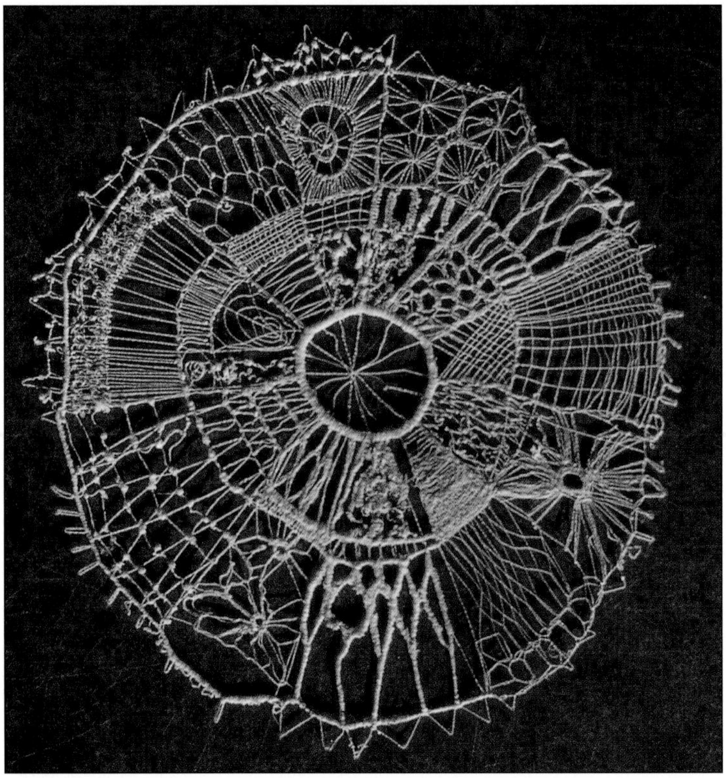

FIGURE 93. AIRBORNE NEEDLE LACE, STIFFENED WITH FABRIC STIFFENER

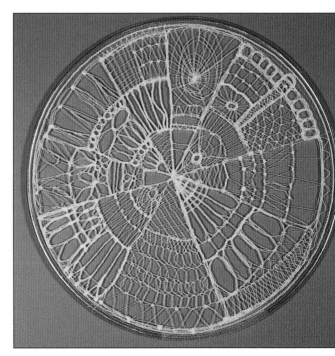

FIGURE 94. STIFFENER IS NOT NEEDED WHEN THE LACE IS WORKED ON A MOUNTING RING.

water, we shall concentrate on the scrim. Since the hoop is unnecessary with the scrim, its handling is quite different. But first we shall begin by creating a circle of lace on a ring with the water-soluble film.

NEEDLE LACE WITH WATER-SOLUBLE STABILIZER

Frame a 14-inch (36-cm) square, double thickness, of water-soluble film in a 10-inch (25.5-cm) hoop. Set your machine for free-machine embroidery (drop the teeth, remove the presser foot). I prefer using either the spring needle or the darning foot for this technique, even though the "fabric" is framed. Place an 8- or 9-inch (20- or 23-cm) metal ring inside the inner hoop.

We shall develop a pattern of lace using primarily straight stitching. Begin at one point on the metal ring. Carefully walk the needle back and forth over the ring, anchoring the thread securely to the ring. Then stitch directly across to the opposite side of the ring, anchoring the thread to the ring the same way in which you began, by walking the needle back and forth several times and locking the thread securely in place. Continue dividing the circle in this way, each time locking the thread to the metal ring.

For variation, instead of stitching across, the presser foot lever may be lifted and the thread simply stretched across the span, again securing it to the opposite edge of the ring. Build up a fairly dense pattern of divided areas as shown in the drawing, then begin stitching in different directions, dividing the areas still further and gradually building up patterns of lace fillings (see figs. 93 and 94). Threads can be clumped, manipulated, and made heavier with zigzag; areas may be changed and dis-

torted as you work. Be sure threads are securely locked where they cross and that all curves are supported by members at right angles to the curve (note the curves in the Battenberg detail, figure 92).

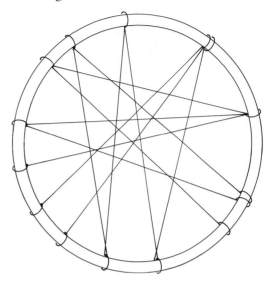

FIGURE 95. SPANNING THREADS FASTENED TO A MOUNTING RING FORM A FOUNDATION FOR LACE FILLINGS.

The stitching becomes almost an engineering exercise, and you will begin to recognize how best to support these different angles of threads as you work with them. Fill some areas with patterns of lace, leave other areas completely open. Remember, this is a splendid opportunity to think in terms of positive and negative spatial relationships. If some areas don't work out the way you wish, simply cut them out, pin another piece of doubled film under the area, and restitch it. Just make sure that all threads are secured firmly to other threads or onto the metal ring. It's an extremely mobile method of developing a composition, and the more you work with it, the more fascinating it becomes!

Don't worry if the water-soluble film rips as you stitch. Extra pieces can be pinned underneath for added support, and since you are securing your stitching to the metal ring as

FIGURE 96. MULTIPLE-RING NEEDLE LACE WORKED ON HEAT-REACTIVE STABILIZER

FIGURE 97. MULTIPLE-RING NEEDLE LACE WORKED ON WATER-SOLUBLE STABILIZER

you work, the stabilizing film becomes less and less necessary. Just make sure that all connections are securely anchored, both thread with thread and thread with metal ring.

When you feel that your circle of lace is completed, hold it up to the light to make sure there are no dangling, unattached threads. Then remove the piece from the hoop and dip the lace circle in water to remove the film. Place it between layers of terry toweling, and pat it dry.

Carefully examine the lace. Nine times out of ten there will be some threads that still are not completely attached, or there are some curved lines that are not supported adequately. Since the lace is mounted on the metal ring, the circle can still be worked. Dangling threads can be carefully caught with the needle and stretched across to meet a stabilizing member. If more support is needed on the edge, again, threads can be caught up with the needle and stretched over to the rim, where they can be adequately walked across and secured. Several threads can be clumped with the zigzag, areas can be changed in shape, and the composition can be further developed even after the film is removed. I've returned to a piece of lace months after finishing it, only to restitch areas, change textures, change concentration of stitches, clump loosened threads, and in general make a completely different (and happily, improved) composition out of the piece that at one time I had considered finished.

SAMPLER 13

NEEDLE LACE WITH HEAT-REACTIVE STABILIZER

For this exercise we shall work on the scrim, eliminating the hoop entirely. Place the metal ring in position on a 12-inch (30.5-cm) square of heat-sensitive scrim, and develop a pattern of lace similar to your work on Sampler 12. This time add heavier threads and beads strung on threads. Build up some heavier areas of stitching by using zigzag and blobs, and by tying knots in laid, couched threads. This is a good way to establish a focal point. Make sure all supporting threads are securely anchored over the metal ring, and that all curves are supported by a network of attached threads.

When the stitching is completed to your satisfaction, place the embroidery on a piece of typing paper, put it on a cookie tin, and bake it approximately 15 minutes in a 300-degree oven or until the scrim chars and crumbles. Remove the piece, cool, and carefully brush away all remnants of the scrim. Make any added repairs that are necessary to stabilize the piece securely on the ring.

Were there any color changes in the threads? Was it possible to remove all charred threads? Did all your materials survive the oven heat? How do you feel this method of stabilization compares with the water-soluble film?

SAMPLER 14
NEEDLE LACE WITH MULTIPLE RINGS

Use the stabilizer of your choice and make another lace circle. This time, in addition to the 9- or 10-inch (23- to 25.5-cm) outer ring, add three smaller rings within the larger one. Overlap the smaller rings in such a way that interesting areas are formed, and design the lace fillings in a way that will enhance the design created by the overlapping rings (see figs. 96 and 97). The collar in figure 98 was stitched on water-soluble film and employed the overlapping rings as a design element. The supporting cords were wrapped by zigzagging over strands of macramé cord.

By this time you've had a chance to explore some of the possibilities of making lace patterns with and without fabric, and by using several different stabilizers. As often happens with machine techniques, we have only scratched the surface of a type of embroidery that offers almost limitless possibilities. I hope that as you worked new ideas were triggered for further exploration and for using these techniques in your own way. The exercises are intended only to suggest further avenues of exploration in the imaginative use of fabrics and threads.

FIGURE 98. *THE SNOW QUEEN'S COLLAR*, NEEDLE LACE STITCHED ON WATER-SOLUBLE FILM

PAINT, INK, AND DYE are the most obvious ways to change the nature of a fabric—so obvious, in fact, that they are often overlooked. There are many good books on the various components and characteristics of paints and dyes. Some are quite technical and perhaps offer more information than the average embroiderer cares to know. Some processes call for a good deal of equipment, and require space that most embroiderers already have filled with fabrics and threads. Therefore I have attempted to limit my approach to using materials readily accessible and easily controlled in the ordinary kitchen or sewing room. After all, our emphasis first and foremost is upon embroidery. The imaginative embroiderer can turn such things as India ink and schoolroom crayons into exciting tools for enhancing stitchery and inspiring new approaches to embroidery. In this chapter we shall explore some of these possibilities.

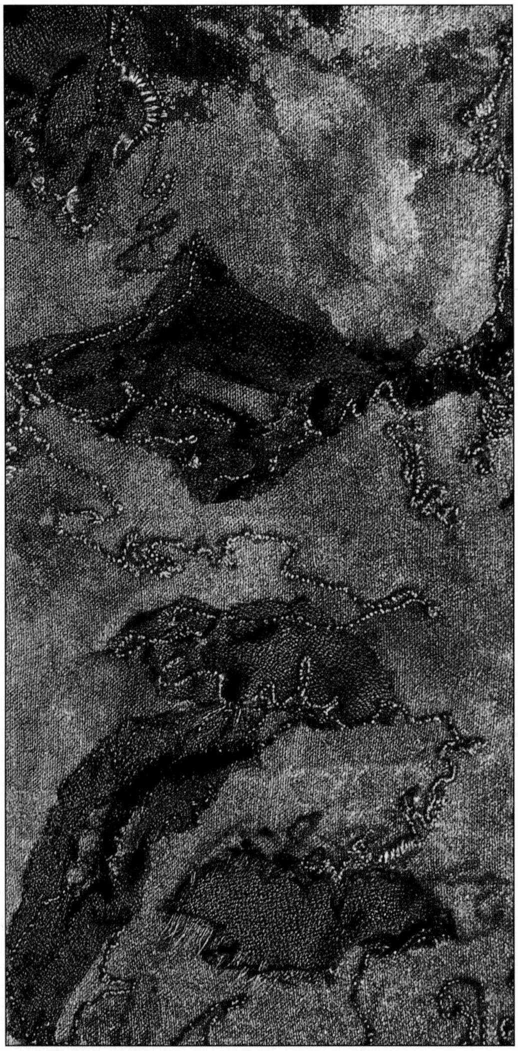

CRAYONS

Most households have a shoebox tucked away somewhere with those dismal short ends of crayons, often so worn and ragged as to make color identification difficult. They were saved for one reason or another, and encaustic is one way to prove them valuable. Encaustic simply means "painted with hot wax." For our experiments, we will not paint, but dip. You'll find that you can use every last scrap and shred of those wretched crayon bits to achieve colorful, random designs that relate beautifully to machine embroidery.

MATERIALS
For this project you will need crayons. If you want to treat yourself to some new ones, try the new metallic crayons. There is a set of golds, silvers, and coppers that add a wonderfully rich, tortoise-shell effect when melted (fig. 99). There is also a range of metallic pastels that are quite different, and equally attractive. The random, accidental nature of the resultant design is particularly compatible with machine embroidery, in this case whipstitch, satin stitch, and a few knots and blobs. You will also need a flat pan or griddle that can be heated (or an electric skillet), aluminum foil, and a variety of fabrics in differing colors and textures.

FIGURE 99. STITCHING WITH METALLIC THREAD IS COMBINED WITH METALLIC CRAYON ENCAUSTIC.

AN EXPERIMENT WITH ENCAUSTIC

Begin with fabric pieces approximately 12 to 15 inches (30 to 38 cm) square, or any size that is easy to handle. Cottons and cotton/polyester blends work well; do not use synthetics or rayon fabrics that will melt with heat.

Cover the inside of the pan with aluminum foil to prevent a build-up of waxy crayon that would be difficult to remove. Heat the pan on the stove to a moderate temperature (or use a moderate setting on an electric skillet). Remove paper from the crayon bits and press them onto the hot surface. As they melt, blobs of hot wax will form, creating interesting shapes in themselves. Fork tines dragged through can produce other patterns. Color distribution can be controlled, and the blobs can be swirled, mixed, and distributed as you choose. Or the color mixture can be completely random. Either way, interesting results will occur. Be sure the wax does not get too hot, as it is highly flammable. Lower the heat if it begins to smoke.

When an interesting pattern of color has formed, use a spoon or wooden handle to carefully press the fabric down into the color. Press, move, and swirl the fabric as fancy dictates. At certain temperatures tiny blobs of wax will spatter out when the fabric is applied, creating small drops that relate beautifully to the stitched knots and blobs.

The nice thing about this method is that you can remove the fabric, examine the effect, then put it back into the color if necessary. New colors can be added, and layers of colors can be built up. Remember that the negative spaces—the unwaxed areas—are just as important as the positives, so choose the pressure areas with that in mind. The hot colors will penetrate most fabrics so that the design can be seen without turning the fabric over.

When the design is complete, press the fabric between layers of newspaper or paper toweling with a hot iron to set the colors and remove excess wax. Several layers of paper might be necessary, depending upon the amount of wax build-up.

As an alternative, roll the fabric between several layers of newspaper and place it in a microwave oven. Microwave at regular speed for two or three minutes, then check. The time will vary according to the thickness of the roll and the power of your oven. Overheating can scorch the fabric. The colors are set when wax has melted and has been absorbed by the paper, and the fabric is hot and steamy. Sometimes several different wrappings will be necessary depending upon the thickness of the wax. This method can also be used for batik (see page 78), and eliminates some of the unpleasant and unhealthy fumes that result from ironing the hot, waxy surface.

By this time your wax design will have suggested some embroidery techniques. I find whip and cable stitches, combined with knots and blobs, are particularly good for relating stitches to encaustic. The mobile, sensitive line of these simple stitches contrasts effectively with the pattern of waxy colors. Area edges can be sharpened through contrasting threads. Areas of color can be emphasized either by outlining or by relating patterns of stitched blobs to the blobs of color. Frame the fabric and stitch. Establish a focal point, and relate the positive areas to negatives through related stitching. Assess your results. Stay stitch the edges of the piece and slip it into a notebook sleeve.

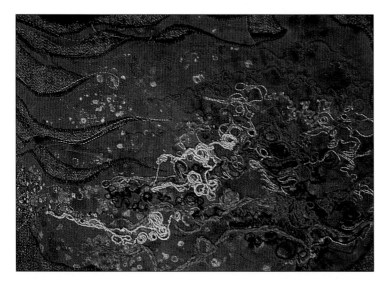

FIGURE 100. STITCHING OVER CRAYON ENCAUSTIC FOR THE FRONT OF A BOOK COVER

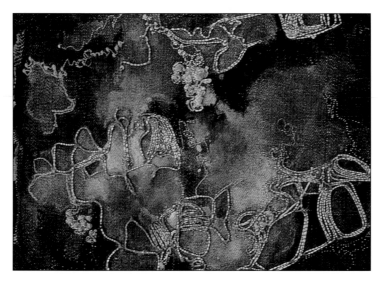

FIGURE 101. THE BACK OF THE BOOK COVER. COUCHING AND CABLE STITCH ADD FURTHER TEXTURE TO THE PIECE.

In *Fire and Ice* (figs. 100 and 101), made as the front and back of a book cover, these techniques have been combined with a small amount of cable stitch, whipstitch, and couching to enhance the texture of the piece. Areas of encaustic were also applied to plain fabric, and the two areas related through stitchery. This alone provides infinite variety.

The black skirt in figure 102 illustrates a similar use of this method. Here, scraps of differ-

ent fabrics were printed with encaustic, cut apart, and used as part of a planned pattern of rectilinear appliqué on a ground fabric. Raw edges of fabric are overlapped and top-stitched throughout, the frayed edges adding subtle texture to the piece. For appliqué to be done this way, extra seam allowance must be added to accommodate the fraying. The stitching uses soft edges as well—single, double, or triple rows of straight stitches that sometimes contrast in color with the fabric, sometimes match, depending upon the linear effect desired.

Lines of straight stitching, echoing the more heavily appliquéd areas toward the bottom, run upward to the waistband, relating the simpler upper area with the more intricately patterned bottom. The focal point is toward the bottom of the skirt, and this area is machine embroidered using straight stitching, a small amount of satin stitching for wider lines, and blobs, which relate well to the textures of the encaustic and enhance the pattern of colors. Washed denim is intro-

FIGURE 102. APPLIQUÉ PIECES FOR THIS SKIRT WERE PRINTED WITH CRAYON ENCAUSTIC.

duced toward the bottom pattern of appliqué, adding weight and further texture as it frays beautifully to provide a heavier fringed effect that complements the lighter weight fabric above, yet adds impact. The embroidery is used primarily to strengthen and give definition to what is suggested by the random encaustic and appliqué (fig. 103). It is a very close harmony of fabric, threads, and crayon that creates an entirely new type of fabric.

FIGURE 103. A DETAIL OF THE APPLIQUÉ SHOWN IN FIGURE 102

SAMPLER 2
FURTHER ENCAUSTIC ADVENTURES

Print several pieces of fabric using the encaustic method described above. Examine the designs and choose the piece that most interests you. Decide where the focal point of this design will occur and plan how this focal point can best be strengthened. Frame the fabric for free machining. Beginning with the focal point, embroider, using a combination of straight stitch and whip-stitch, knots and blobs. Carefully consider your design as you work, pulling forward the important areas, pushing back the lesser ones, until you are satisfied that it works as a composition. Finish the edges and slip into a notebook sleeve.

Another encaustic technique involves water-soluble film and the cutwork method described on page 57. The random nature of the encaustic design suggests interesting shapes that might be cut out (and perhaps applied elsewhere in the composition), backed with the film, then worked with lace to pick up the overall motion and feeling of the design. This process contributes immeasurably to the concept of creating new fabrics from the ordinary ones at hand.

SAMPLER 3
ENCAUSTIC WITH LACE

Select another piece of encaustic fabric and frame it for free machining. Determine where the focal point will occur and cut out an interesting shape. Save this cut-out for future use. Pin a piece of water-soluble film behind this opening and stitch an area of lace (see page 54) to create a focal point, carefully relating the areas and lines of the lace to those of the surrounding fabric pattern. Some slit-fabric techniques may also be employed here (see fig. 88). Enhance the lace and fabric lines further with couching, choosing heavier threads that will relate well to the concept of the lace. You might also cut strips of the encaustic printed fabric and use these strips instead of heavier threads and yarns. Edges can be turned back or rolled; beads can be strung on the strips, and knots tied at intervals to relate to the beads.

When the embroidery has been completed, remove it from the hoop and either spray with water or dip to remove the film. Cut the edges of the encaustic to roughly follow the outer edges of the pattern. Mount the piece on another piece of fabric, placing it in such a way that the cut-out area works as part of the composition. Some of the cuts could be used in conjunction with the cut-out to apply elsewhere on the ground fabric. Strips of the printed fabric can be added and manipulated. In other words, you are now creating an entirely new piece combining the lace-focused encaustic and other bits and pieces arranged strategically to form a pleasing composition and an entirely different type of fabric.

Finish the edges and slip the piece into a sleeve for your notebook. Considering the characteristics of the two types of stabilizers discussed above, why did we use the water-soluble film here, rather than the scrim?

ENCAUSTIC TO WEAR

Encaustic is a natural for wearable art, and never fails to attract attention. The gold shirt in figure 104 demonstrates the versatility of the technique. Encaustic dyed fabric was applied to a purchased shirt, embroidered in straight and whipstitches with knots and blobs, then enriched with couched threads and antique buttons. Soft-edge appliqué is used throughout. Areas of the fabric were positioned to enhance the natural cut of the shirt, both back and front, and were extended down onto the sleeve. It's a garment that is exciting, comfortable, distinctive, and a delight to wear.

MATERIALS
You will need one sweatshirt, in a color you particularly enjoy wearing. A hard-surfaced, firmer weave fabric is ideally suited to this purpose. Some shirts have a stone-washed finish that relates beautifully to encaustic and stitchery. You will also need approximately 1 yard (1 m) of harmonizing fabric(s) to be used for encaustic.

SAMPLER 4
AN ENCAUSTIC SHIRT
Dye the accent fabrics using the encaustic method described above. Make them all one color, or a harmonizing variety. For use in garments I suggest putting your pieces of encaustic through a quick washer/dryer cycle. You will lose a bit of color intensity, but you will know exactly what strength of hues you are dealing with as you plan the embroidery. For the gold shirt (fig. 104) I used some well-worn denim from old jeans, since I knew I would wear the shirt with denim jeans and skirts.

Use your vocabulary of stitches to machine embroider areas of the encaustic, emphasizing certain places more than others. Work with threads that pick up colors of both the shirt and the encaustic fabrics.

When you feel the embroidery is fairly complete (you can always add more), lay out the shirt and start thinking in terms of shapes that will enhance the cut of the shirt. Some of them have set-in sleeves, some have slanted raglans. Mine has a special seam extending from the shoulder down one-third the length of the sleeve, then back again, forming a definite area for design consideration. Some shirts have yokes or pockets. Some have rounded necks, some have front placket closures. All these features should be analyzed and taken into consideration when planning design areas that will best enhance your shirt.

At this point you can back the encaustic fabric with an iron-on adhesive. Keep in mind, however, that if the adhesive is applied now, you will be able to use only the right side of your encaustic fabric. If you plan to use the reverse side in some cases (and this can be helpful in arranging your appliqué), then apply the adhesive after the pieces have been cut and arranged.

A simple way to stay a small area before stitching is to slip a small piece of transparent kitchen wrap under the area, and fuse it with the iron (be careful not to touch the iron to the wrap). This stay is temporary, but will hold until the stitching is completed. It is more difficult to stay all the uneven edges with this method. At times this is advantageous, for you are free to curl, fold, and manipulate those edges as you stitch, adding to the versatility of the applied fabrics and contributing a good deal to the texture of the piece.

The next step is to be bold and brave, and simply cut the encaustic fabric into large, free-form areas, more or less following the contours of the design. Vary the size and shape of the pieces. Now spread out your shirt and start arranging and rearranging the pieces to create an interesting composition. I slip my shirt over one of the cardboard shirt forms available in craft shops, but a stiff magazine works just as well, allowing pins to be set into the fabrics as you work. Consider the areas that can best be accented, given your own body shape. I usually concentrate on the area around the neck and over the shoulders, with some vertical emphasis down the front and back. A tall, thin person might use a strong border design just above the lower edge, continuing it upward with a series of interesting shapes.

Further stitching can be done without opening seams of the shirt. If you want heavy sleeve emphasis that will involve a good deal of free machining, I suggest carefully opening the underarm seam of each sleeve so you can work with a hoop.

Remember as you plan your design to allow some shirt fabric to show through. This way, the ground fabric of the shirt becomes an important element in the composition (that

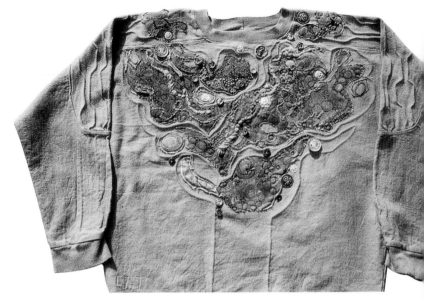

FIGURE 104. A SHIRT OF SOFT GOLD DENIM IS ENHANCED WITH ENCAUSTIC, ACHINE EMBROIDERY, PINTUCKING, AND BEADS.

old positive/negative relationship again). This is a very free and exciting stage of your project. Try moving the pieces in all directions, cutting apart, rearranging, overlapping. Cut out some interesting small shapes—circles, oval, free-form areas—and place the cut-outs elsewhere on the shirt. This will add to the feeling of related shapes, which in turn will strengthen and provide unity for your design.

When the arrangement is complete, if you have bonded the applied fabrics or secured them with plastic wrap, simply go over with a hot iron to hold the appliqués in place. This is a temporary bond, but it will secure the appliqués until they have been stitched. Should you change your mind about positioning, slight changes can be made by re-ironing the area and lifting it while still warm. A slight adhesive residue will remain, so use this remedy only when absolutely necessary.

Now comes the fun! Choose stitches to anchor the applied shapes and to enrich the overall design of the shirt. Work the stitching in such a way that it unifies the pieces, relates them to the shirt itself, and still forms a dramatic focal point to really give the design strength. It is not necessary to finish all edges with a hard, closely worked satin stitch. Softer edges, by way of contrast, can be stitched with a series of straight-stitched lines, following, echoing, and emphasizing the lines of the appliqué. Heavier threads and yarns can be couched. I find that narrow strips of the encaustic fabric work well for couching. Narrow strips, straight-stitched down the center, respond in interesting ways and serve as a good transitional element between fabric and threads. In some places I folded up the edge of the applied piece (no adhesive under that particular edge), which added dimensional interest to the appliqué (fig. 105).

FIGURE 105. COUCHED FABRIC STRIPS AND HEAVY YARN ADD DIMENSION AND TEXTURE TO THE SHIRT SHOWN ON THE PRECEDING PAGE.

Strengthen the focal point with some found objects—I used lots of old buttons, judiciously placed to create a focal point. I further related my stitching to the lines of the garment by bringing parallel lines of double-needle pintucking down that sleeve section. Pintucking was also used within the embroidered areas.

You may find it a bit awkward at first to place the hoop properly since you will work through the neck and bottom openings of the shirt, but it's not terribly difficult. If your machine has a free-arm bed, it will help you maneuver more easily. Difficult places can always be stitched with a presser foot and without a hoop. Free machining can be done with the darning foot or spring needle, and the hoop won't be needed. There's always a way to do it if you take time to really know your machine and its capabilities.

This form of appliqué can, of course, be done on skirts, cardigans, tote bags, and scarves. One idea leads to another, and that's what it's all about.

COLORING WITH CRAYONS

Perhaps you have allowed yourself the luxury of a new box of crayons (beautiful things in themselves), evoking memories of first days of school and new schoolbags, pencils and tablets. Everyday crayons can be used directly on fabric. Then to set the color, place the fabric between layers of paper padding, and press with a hot iron. You will achieve a distinctive texture and quality of color that works very well with machine embroidery. The normal stroke of the crayon produces a very distinctive and pleasing texture.

If you wish to specialize, try fabric crayons. There are two kinds, both available in art supply and stationery shops. Read labels carefully. One type is recommended only for synthetic fibers, the other only for natural fibers, and their permanence depends upon choosing the proper one for your fabric. In the case of blends of natural and synthetic fabric, use a combination of the two.

Both kinds of fabric crayons are heat set, and both can be used directly on the fabric or can be worked first on paper, then transferred to fabric with a hot iron. As with schoolroom crayons, textures that result are quite distinctive and different from those achieved with a brush and paint or ink, and they harmonize well with the stitchery.

One major consideration is that the colors look quite different in the stick than they do on fabric, so I would recommend doing a trial run or sampler before beginning any project. Fabric crayons are also softer and waxier than schoolroom variety, and more care must be taken in handling them. Because of this softer quality, fine, sharp lines are impossible, but since crisp, fine line is an important characteristic of machine embroidery, the techniques complement each other nicely.

Elliot's Quilt (fig. 31) illustrates how fabric crayons were combined with machine embroidery and appliqué to suggest a child-like, stylized concept of the Biblical story. The rainbow and some of the flowers were done in crayon, after the fashion of a child's use of color in simple areas, which relates beautifully with the strong, direct simplicity of the appliqué. In this case the crayons were used directly on the fabric.

A supplementary method of using fabric crayons is illustrated in *Smugglers' Cave* (figs. 54 and 55). One of the objects of this panel was to use all the colors of the spectrum, beginning with yellow at the focal point (the treasure trove), and progressing outward in concentric blocks of distorted log cabin strip piecing. I needed a particular hue of yellow-orange which I couldn't find in fabric. By applying a light coating of red crayon over a predominantly yellow printed fabric, the desired hue of yellow-orange was achieved.

SAMPLER 5
CRAYONS: DIRECT APPLICATION

Make a series of small samples, each approximately 4 inches (10 cm) square, and take

notes on each sample. Experiment with the different kinds of crayons available to you, using the kind that suits your fabric. Heat set the samples. Notice the different qualities of texture, the color changes, and spread of color (this can vary with the amount of pigment you have used). Note variables and think how these characteristics can become advantages when combined with embroidery. Keep these samples in a partitioned plastic sleeve in your notebook as a valuable ready-reference.

SAMPLER 6
CRAYONS: HEAT-TRANSFERRED DESIGNS

You'll find that using fabric crayons in conjunction with embroidery is more successful when simple areas are involved. The detail and delineation come with the embroidery. We'll experiment with simple, geometric shapes in an overlapped print.

On a piece of typing paper color an interesting design of rectangles. Use a variety of proportions and sizes. Space them at differing intervals but don't overlap them. Experiment with mixing different colors of crayons within the same area. Make some areas heavier than others.

On a second sheet of paper, do the same with circles, concentrating on an interesting relationship between positive and negative areas, and variety of color. Color some circles more heavily than others.

Place the first sheet of paper face down on a piece of light-valued fabric and press with a medium-hot iron. Lift a corner of the paper to see if the print is completed, taking care not to move it. When you are satisfied with the print, remove this paper and position the second sheet on the same fabric. Set the color. You will now see an interesting pattern of overlapping geometric shapes. New tones and areas will be formed where shapes overlap, adding to the interest of color, value, and design.

Place an embroidery hoop over the fabric, moving it until the most pleasing relationship of positive and negative shapes is within the circle. Frame it for free-machining. Apply your own vocabulary of stitches to strengthen and complete the composition suggested by the crayoned shapes. This is an interesting way of developing a random, accidental design into something new and exciting. It will challenge your knowledge of stitches as well as sharpen your design perception. It's fun! Stay stitch the edges of your piece and slip into a plastic sleeve.

WORKING WITH INK

India ink can always be found in stationery and art supply shops. Its color is strong and permanent, particularly in black, and it is available in a small range of hues as well. The transparent inks work well on fabrics, and they are water-soluble until dry. The hues can be layered on fabric to create different tones. Do not attempt to mix new tones by combining the inks, however; only muddied tones will result.

India inks can be applied with brushes, or with the pen filler attached to the underside of the cap. The filler

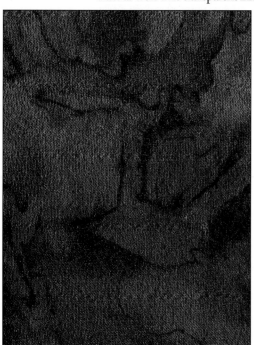

FIGURE 106. FOR THIS DESIGN, INDIA INK WAS APPLIED TO WET FABRIC.

can be used like a pen itself, producing a strong, mobile line that relates beautifully to machine embroidery. I find these inks are most successful when applied to wet fabrics.

For an interesting textural effect, sprinkle some coarse salt on the wet inked area. When the piece is dry, just brush away the excess. This kind of design is quite free. The spread of the ink can be only partially controlled, but chance effects can be highly distinctive. Success with this medium, then, depends a great deal upon the sensitivity and imagination of the embroiderer in using it as a springboard for creative stitchery. It's an exciting and challenging approach to design.

The peacock design shown in figure 80 was worked with India inks and salt. A purchased sweatshirt was thoroughly soaked in water, then wadded up and manipulated into interesting ridges and contoured areas. I placed a pad of newspapers inside the shirt to separate front from back, and a roll of newspaper inside each sleeve to prevent ink from bleeding from one side of the garment to the other. The paper absorbed excess water and helped keep the surfaces wet. I used a brush and the cap applicator, and emphasized the contours, applying ink liberally along the ridges and allowing it to bleed and run into the hollows of the manipulated fabric (fig. 106). The shirt was left in this position until it was almost dry.

At this point the shirt was smoothed out and important lines and areas were reemphasized with ink. Because greatest ink penetration was in the wettest areas, the strength of the color was diminished in those places. The piece was allowed to dry completely.

The peacock feather design was drawn on water-soluble film with a permanent felt-tip pen and pinned in place on the shirt. A hoop was used to work the embroidery. A combination of regular and metallic threads was used for the stitching, suggesting the iridescent quality of the feather. The shirt was dipped in water to remove the film.

A black, waterproof felt-tip pen was successful in this instance for marking on the film. This is not always the case. I stitched a beige shirt with a rather intricate cutwork and lace pattern (fig. 107), which I had marked on water-soluble film, framed up, then stitched through both film and fabric. When I removed the film I discovered that the threads had picked up a slightly bluish residue from the marking pen. I tried everything I could think of to remove this tinge, but it remains today. It is not unsightly, but neither is it white. So I would suggest that you always use a white paint pen that is made specifically for marking on the water-soluble film.

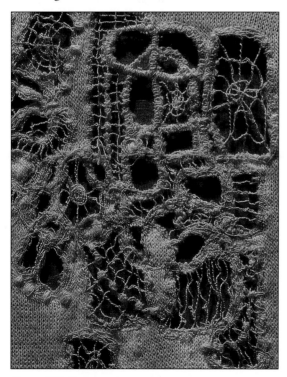

FIGURE 107. CUTWORK AND NEEDLE LACE WORKED ON A KNIT SHIRT WITH WATER-SOLUBLE FILM

SAMPLER 7
INK EFFECTS

You'll find that the fabric itself makes quite a difference in how ink reacts, so our first experiment should be with fabrics. Assemble a variety of plain fabrics, some lightweight and some as heavy as sweatshirt knit. Cut pieces about 12 inches (30 cm) square for easy manipulation, and for framing later in a 10-inch (25.5-cm) hoop.

Wet each piece thoroughly. Working on a heavy pad of newspaper, manipulate, rearrange, form contours in pleasing designs, then reinforce these contours with ink as described above. Remember, the ink is reduced in strength by the dampness in the fabric. The color will lighten as the fabric dries. Experiment with degrees of dampness as well as ink quantity. Allow the pieces to dry in place. When

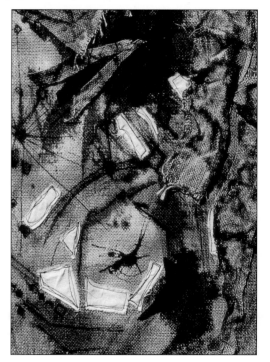

FIGURE 108. AN INDIA INK DESIGN ON BURLAP IS ENHANCED WITH EMBROIDERY AND APPLIQUÉ.

they are dry, reinforce and strengthen with ink any lines or areas necessary to the effectiveness of the design.

Now think about the stitching. Choose a favorite piece, or stitch pieces of several fabrics together in a patchwork. Frame it in a hoop for free-motion embroidery, and stitch. Figure 108 illustrates the use of this method

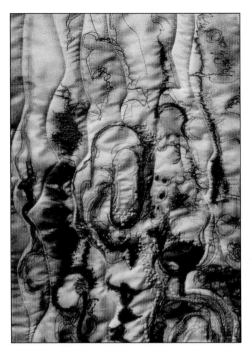

FIGURE 109. INDIA INK AND SALT CREATED THIS SPECIAL EFFECT ON BLEACHED MUSLIN.

on burlap; in figure 109 it was used on unbleached muslin.

For future reference, keep samples of all these fabrics as a record of the way each reacts to ink. Slip the small samples into partitioned plastic pages, along with any notes and comments you have made. Finish the edges of the embroidered piece and add to your notebook.

BATIK WITH PAINT

Batik is a wax resist process that has been used for centuries in India, Indonesia, and Asia in general. The principle is simple: A design is painted or drawn on fabric with wax (or some other resist material), the fabric is dyed, and the wax is removed. This process can be repeated many times to build up layers of color. After each dyeing, new wax is applied to retain an area of that particular color.

One of the most distinctive characteristics of batik is the crackled texture which results from breaks in the surface of the wax that allow dye to penetrate the fabric underneath. It is this which provides delightful inspiration for machine embroidery. The extent of this effect is easy to control. The more brittle the wax, the more crackle occurs when the fabric is manipulated or folded. This quality of the wax is easy to control. Many batik artists prefer a combination of ordinary paraffin wax (the

kind one buys at the grocery store to pour on top of homemade jelly) and beeswax, which is harder to find and more expensive. I find that paraffin wax mixed with some petroleum jelly works very well. A greater proportion of paraffin results in a brittle wax; more petroleum jelly makes it softer and less crackly.

Originally I melted wax in a tin can, squashed in at the sides to form a pouring spout, sitting in a pan of hot water on the stove. I was lucky. Hot wax is very flammable and can easily overheat and burst into flame. A much safer and more successful method is to line an electric skillet with aluminum foil and melt the wax in that. At a rummage sale, I bought a very inexpensive skillet that is kept exclusively for batik. The temperature can be controlled and even the widest brush can be dipped into it. Even wadded-up fabric can be dipped directly into the pan—with rather interesting results. After the wax has dried on the fabric, excess blobs can be brushed or peeled off into the skillet and used again.

There are a number of ways to apply wax to fabric. Beautiful wooden or metal printing blocks once were used for the purpose, dipped into hot wax and pressed onto the fabric. Some can still be found in flea markets and antique shops. Traditional djanting tools are available in art supply shops in sizes ranging from very fine to quite heavy. A fascinating tool, it consists of a metal cup fixed on top of a fine, hollow tube. The cup is filled with hot wax, which flows as a controlled stream to create a line on the fabric. Many different effects can be created with the djanting tool, but proper control of it does require some practice.

Then there are the modern electric versions. Electric djanting tools maintain very even heat and are finer and easier to use, but of course are more expensive to buy.

The traditional tools are fun to see and fun to experiment with, but not essential. There are much simpler ways to apply wax to your fabric.

Cheap brushes in a variety of sizes work well. I emphasize cheap because good quality brushes would be ruined by the hot wax. Dime store synthetic bristle brushes work fine. They can be used to paint wax onto the fabric in streams or blobs of various sizes. An old toothbrush loaded with hot wax and flipped across the fabric makes a lovely spatter pattern. A stick swirled in wax and run across the fabric makes a textured line. Ordinary kitchen utensils can be brought into play provided you don't object to a coating of wax on them. When this happens, place the object on a pad of paper toweling and put it in a gas oven. The heat from the pilot light will soften the wax, making it easy to wipe off.

A lighted candle makes an interesting pattern of wax when tilted and moved over the surface of the fabric. Be careful not to touch the fabric with the flame. This is not a great problem, because you'll find the flame always flickers upward, away from the fabric, when the candle is tilted downward. This is a handy and very easy way to create wax patterns, but lacks the control that is possible with a brush.

For a different texture, rub an unlighted candle end over the fabric. This takes a good deal of pressure and wax build-up, but the rough texture suggests all kinds of interesting stitchery. After a design is painted, printed, or drawn with wax, the fabric can be wadded up or folded to crackle the wax. This will produce the fine lines running through the design that are so distinctive in batik. The amount of cracking can be controlled by the amount of fabric manipulation after waxing, as well as by the make-up of the wax. Next, the piece is either dipped into dye, or paint is applied.

Fiber-reactive dyes that can be dissolved in cold water are well-suited to batik; hot-water dyes would melt the wax prematurely. The dyes then are heat set. They are available in a wide range of colors in most art supply shops. Many can be used only on natural fiber fabrics. Be sure to read the directions carefully as these dyes do require a special mixing procedure. These are true dyes which penetrate the molecular structure of the fabric and are permanent when handled correctly.

If you feel you don't want to become involved in this sort of process, a much easier coloring medium is ordinary acrylic paint. This is a paint rather than a dye, hence it does not become part of the fibers themselves. It works very well as a basis for embroidery. It is cold-water based, easily applied, easily mixed, and readily available. It stiffens the fabric to a certain degree, depending upon its concentration, and this can be an advantage for machining as it gives more body to the fabric. I find, too, that the fabric becomes more flexible as the embroidery progresses.

With either dye or paint, layers of color and pattern can be developed. In both cases, a wax design is applied to the fabric, the paint or dye is applied, and the fabric is allowed to dry. Air drying is necessary; heat drying would melt the wax and destroy the design. But a hair dryer—on the "cool" temperature setting—can speed the process. After the fabric is dry, another pattern of wax is applied, the color is again added, and the process continued until the pattern of color is complete to your satisfaction. Remember, any area of color that you wish to retain must be covered with wax before the next color is added.

A friend of mine once decided to experiment with simple flour paste as a resist. The day was warm and sunny, and she spread her fab-

FIGURE 110. FABRIC DYE WAS PAINTED ONTO THE FABRIC FOR THIS BATIK.

ric out on the grass to dry between color applications. A bit later she discovered that the local squirrel and chipmunk populations found the flour paste very tasty. A piece of naturally distressed, well-manipulated fabric was the result. This drawback aside, flour paste actually works quite well and is easy to come by. It produces a slightly different texture.

Traditionally, the final step of removing the wax was accomplished by boiling the fabric in huge, outdoor vats. The boiling water removes the wax and sets the dye. We don't all have access to boiling cauldrons in our back gardens, but there are alternatives. The fabric can be ironed, sandwiched between thick layers of paper to absorb the wax. The microwave method (described on page 69) is also an option. In any event, be sure to have plenty of paper on hand to absorb the wax. Try to avoid inhaling the fumes from the hot wax. A well-ventilated room is advisable both for dyeing and removing the wax.

Many fabrics can be used for batik, but do check the fiber content specifications of your paints or dyes. An advantage of acrylics is they'll work on any fiber. I find unbleached muslin an all-time favorite for batik. It is inexpensive—one can use yards of it without feeling guilty—and it works well for stitching. As an alternative, use the stronger parts of your worn-out sheets, or pick up some inexpensive ones at a rummage sale. Figure 110 shows an example of unbleached muslin batiked with painted-on fabric dye. Figure 111 shows the yoke of a caftan made from unbleached muslin and batiked with fiber-reactive dyes,

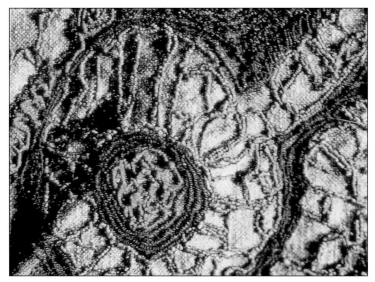

FIGURE 111. WHIPSTITCH ACCENTS A BATIK DESIGN COLORED WITH FIBER-REACTIVE DYE.

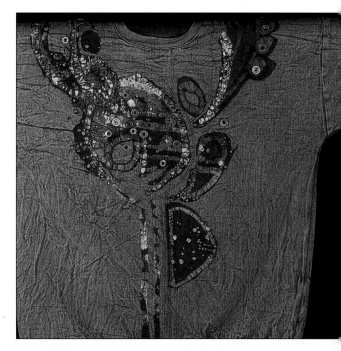

FIGURE 112. DYED BATIK IS USED AS APPLIQUÉ ON THIS SHIRT, THE DESIGN HIGHLIGHTED WITH COUCHING AND ANTIQUE BUTTONS.

FIGURE 113. A DETAIL OF THE SHIRT IN FIGURE 112

then embroidered. Figure 112 shows a commercial denim sweatshirt enhanced with appliqué of embroidered batik (dyed with fiber-reactive dyes), couched threads, manipulated fabric edges, and antique buttons (fig. 113). This is the same procedure described for Sampler 4 (page 72) except that encaustic was used rather than batik.

Many other textures and weights of fabrics will work. Don't hesitate to experiment, and keep swatches and notes of all experiments for future reference.

ADDITIONAL SUPPLIES

One block of paraffin wax; jar of petroleum jelly; set of acrylic paints; inexpensive synthetic bristle brushes in small, medium, and large sizes; stack of newspaper; container for melting wax; small set of liquid transfer dyes.

SAMPLER 8

EXPERIMENTS WITH BATIK

This sampler involves making several smaller ones to keep in your notebook as a reference. Use 4-inch (10-cm) fabric squares and experiment with different patterns of wax and layers

of acrylics. You will find that the color sequence affects the nature of the color scheme. Experiment with this as well as with different methods of applying the wax. Keep your samples, along with notes and comments, in partitioned plastic sleeves.

The crackled texture of batik lends itself well to machine embroidery. A very handsome design can be worked by simply delineating the crackles with straight stitching. Whipstitch can add a second color and more texture as well, and cable adds still more texture. Since the waxed design is the same on both sides of the fabric, it can easily be cable stitched from the wrong side.

Couching adds another dimension through the use of heavier threads, raised knots, and beads strung on threads or fabric strips to be knotted and manipulated as they are couched down. And don't overlook the possibilities of cutting out and rearranging shapes, or applying other fabrics to enhance the batik design. The freeform nature of many batik designs lends itself well to padding and free quilting, too. Figures 114 and

FIGURE 114. APPLIED AND PADDED AREAS OF BATIK ARE RELATED TO A GROUND FABRIC WITH STITCHING.

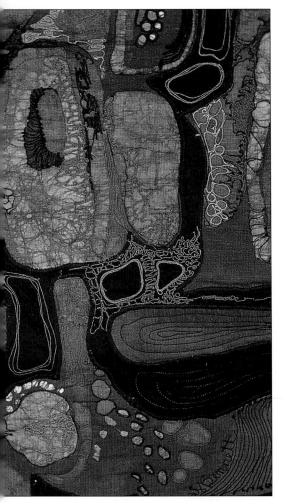

FIGURE 115. A DETAIL OF FIGURE 114, SHOWING THE USE OF WHIPSTITCH AND BLOBS

115 show an example worked this way.

In other words, keep in mind your entire vocabulary of machine techniques. Let the design of the batiked fabric trigger that vocabulary into making new and exciting statements.

■

SAMPLER 9

BATIK PATCHWORK

There are many good books on traditional batik, many of which involve multiple dye baths, a number of containers, a good deal of equipment, and plenty of table space. As machine embroiderers, we shall approach the technique in a less traditional manner.

Assemble 12-inch (30-cm) squares of fabric in harmonious colors. Include unbleached muslin, a slub-woven heavier fabric, velveteen, and corduroy. I like to work in my kitchen, on a drawing board padded with layers of newspaper laid across an open drawer near the sink. The water source is handy, and the choice of the right drawer allows the board to be placed at a level where the entire piece can be viewed from above.

Use melted wax, brushes of various sizes, and any other tools you'd like to try. Apply wax in interesting areas and lines to all the fabrics. Leave plenty of open space for future layers of wax.

Paint the fabrics with acrylic colors, thinning them with water to a consistency that will spread easily on each particular type of fabric. Begin with the colors of lightest values. Light values can be achieved either by mixing with white or thinning with water. Don't hesitate to paint right over the waxed areas. Lift each wet piece onto a stack of fresh newspaper to dry while working with the next fabric.

When all pieces are dry, apply a second pattern of wax. Be very free with the wax and explore its possibilities. Don't try to control it, but let it flow freely. Apply another layer of paints, this time using darker values. Continue this process until you think you have built up interesting patterns of wax and paint. The layers will eventually be quite thick.

The nice thing about this very free approach is that even after removing the wax, if you feel the need for something more, the wax/paint layering can be continued. Obviously, each time more paint is added, colors, tones, and values will change. This is the fun of accidental designing. Eventually you will learn to control not only edges and lines, but to predict quite accurately the various color effects. But your first effort is definitely an experimental piece. Explore it to its limits.

Remove the wax by first peeling or brushing the excess back into the melting pot. Then either iron the fabric between layers of paper padding, or roll it in layers of paper and put it in the microwave. I use a regular-speed microwave, and test after every few seconds. Once I left a piece in too long and it scorched a bit, but even that resulted in an interesting color change. If you do scorch a hole in the fabric, don't worry. Cut out around it and apply another piece of fabric, or work needle lace in the area. A truly creative person takes advantage of every mistake and turns it into something exciting!

Don't worry if the nap of the velveteen and corduroy becomes flattened during this process. With paint and wax application it is unavoidable. The textures are quite interesting, even if they no longer resemble the original fabrics.

After the wax has been removed, cut one of the fabrics into a five-sided piece approximately 4 inches (10 cm) across. The five sides can be of unequal length. From the remaining pieces of fabric, cut strips of varying widths and lengths.

Piece the strips onto the sides of the pentagon in a log cabin sequence (see fig. 41). Proceed around the circumference in a clockwise direction, making sure that the next strip covers the entire width of the previous one. As mentioned previously, the traditional log cabin quilt block pattern begins with a square and is developed in equal-width strips around that square, with strips pieced right sides together, seams on the wrong side. For variety we are working with a five-sided center. For greater variety still, and more interesting edges, piece some of the strips with wrong sides together, allowing a soft, raw seam to show. Press this seam open.

Mix colors, textures, and pattern as the piecing progresses. Piece strips as necessary to fill out the length or width. Continue until most of the printed fabric has been used in an irregular, five-sided shape.

Frame the piece in a hoop. Accent a focal point and related areas with carefully chosen free machining. Don't hesitate to add found objects or heavy couched threads. Overlay

extra pieces for additional textures, contrasting hard and soft edges. These areas can relate well to the soft-edged seams above.

The stitching must necessarily be carefully placed and have a fairly simple color scheme since so much color is in the fabric. I suggest you choose one color from the fabric that seems to dominate, and emphasize this with the embroidery. Equal proportions of many colors become dull and uninteresting. One dominant color with several subordinate ones is much more exciting.

With this exercise you have created an entirely new piece of fabric that could be mounted as a hanging or picture. It might also be squared off for use on a special pillow or tote bag. As you experiment with creating new fabrics, think how they could be put to use in enjoyable ways. Using your art is almost as much fun as creating it!

WORKING WITH DYE

Dye differs from paint primarily in that it penetrates the actual molecules of the fibers rather than simply coloring the surface of the fabric. It has the advantage of being a good deal more permanent, especially important if the piece will be washed and dried repeatedly. It is more stable in sunlight. The disadvantages are that it is usually more expensive, sometimes more difficult to find, and requires more care in handling. There are more fabric dyes available to the fiber artist than ever before, and it can be used successfully if directions on the package are followed carefully.

There are two major types of dye. One is designed to be used directly on the fabric, applied by dipping or brushing. The other is a transfer dye that is painted in reverse on paper, then transferred with a hot iron to the fabric.

Dye colors look quite different in the bottle than they look after they've been heat-set on fabric. One kind is actually clear, developing color only after exposure to sunlight.

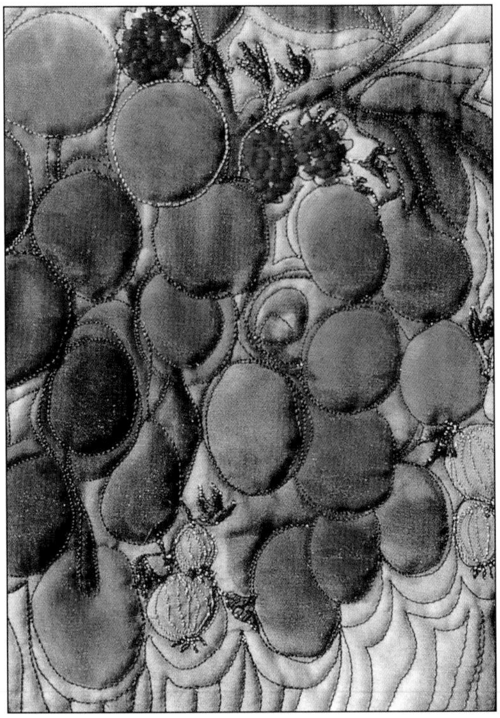

Many dyes are specifically intended for use on fabrics with a particular fiber content; therefore it is critical to read labels before buying. Some work only on natural fibers, some only on synthetics. Some are compatible with both.

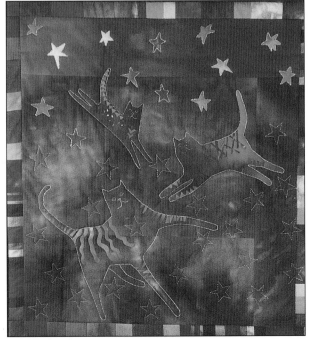

FIGURE 116. FABRIC FOR THE *GRAPE TUNIC* WAS PAINTED WITH TRANSFER DYES.

Special dyes are made for use only on silk and require steam setting, which can necessitate additional equipment. With any dye, it is advisable to make test strips.

When you paint with dyes, the liquid is more difficult to contain within prescribed areas. Some dyes require special blocking agents, sold with the dyes, for delineating areas and creating lines. With these, interesting cloisonné or stained-glass window effects can be achieved.

Dyes can be used for direct surface color, transfer color, or for batik. The sleeve detail of the *Grape Tunic* (fig.116) was painted directly with fabric transfer dyes. Melody Johnson's *Cats in Space* (fig. 117) was constructed from dyed fabric, then machine quilted. Figure 110 shows an example of batik using layers of transfer dyes painted directly onto the fabric to produce strong, intense colors.

SAMPLER 10

AN EXPERIMENT WITH TRANSFER DYEING

One distinctive quality of the transfer dye method is its transparency, which can result in interesting overlay effects. The *Bog Box* (fig. 118) was printed using two transparent transfers, then hand embroidered with simple stitches. It could as well have been done on the machine.

Begin with two pieces of white or light-colored fabric approximately 12 by 15 inches (30 by 38 cm), and two pieces of typing paper or newsprint the same size. On one piece of paper compose a simple landscape design consisting of sky at the top (with clouds, if you wish), fields in the mid-ground, and a stream of water across the foreground. Remember that the design will be reversed when it is

FIGURE 117. HAND-DYED FABRICS WERE USED FOR *CATS IN SPACE*, BY MELODY JOHNSON.

FIGURE 118. THE *BOG BOX* WAS PAINTED WITH TRANSFER DYES, THEN STITCHED.

printed. Consider carefully a pleasing proportion and distribution of these three areas.

Using a transfer dye compatible with your fabric, paint these elements. They need not be heavily colored, just suggested. Experiment with blending the colors (fig. 119). On the second piece of paper, plan a foreground to be laid on over the first piece. Mentally divide the area roughly into thirds, as you did above, and add trees against the sky. Consider their placement, height, overlapping branches, and other features. Don't hesitate to allow trunks to extend down into the area of fields. Avoid fine detail; rather, lay in the color freely, simply, and roughly to suggest the texture of tree bark. Try combining different values and tones of browns and greens.

In the middle area, create a pattern of vertical lines to suggest an underbrush of weeds and wild plants and flowers. Combine colors, vary the brush strokes, and strive for interesting angles and heights. Keep the design spontaneous and simple; details and emphasis will be provided by the stitching. In other words,

you are creating an atmosphere with the paints, hinting at an environment or situation that will be more fully developed with embroidery. In the lower part suggest water plants, weeds, and perhaps even some fish.

When the two paper designs are completed, it is time to print. Place the first pattern face down on the fabric and press carefully with a medium-hot dry iron. Lift a corner of the pattern to check the strength of the print, but try not to move the pattern. If the print is satisfactory, remove this pattern and position the second design face down over the first, roughly aligning the three areas of both. Don't be concerned if they don't align exactly; areas that are slightly blurred or overlapped can create new and interesting effects. Transfer with iron as above, again testing for strength of print.

Examine the results. Notice the color changes that have occurred between the painted elements and the printed. If the weed area is not as heavily textured as you wish, try moving the second pattern slightly to the right or left and make a third print over the second. Most

FIGURE 119. AREAS PAINTED WITH TRANSFER DYE, BEFORE PRINTING

patterns can be successfully printed several times, often with interesting variations in texture and value intensities.

After printing is completed, frame the fabric for free machining. Establish emphasis or a focal point, perhaps the fish in the water, one or two trees near the center of the composition, or an interesting clump of weeds or wildflowers. Most people seem to be comfortable if the focal point is slightly above or below center, and off a bit to the right or left, but choose the place you wish to emphasize and work the embroidery accordingly. You will find the verticals and textures of

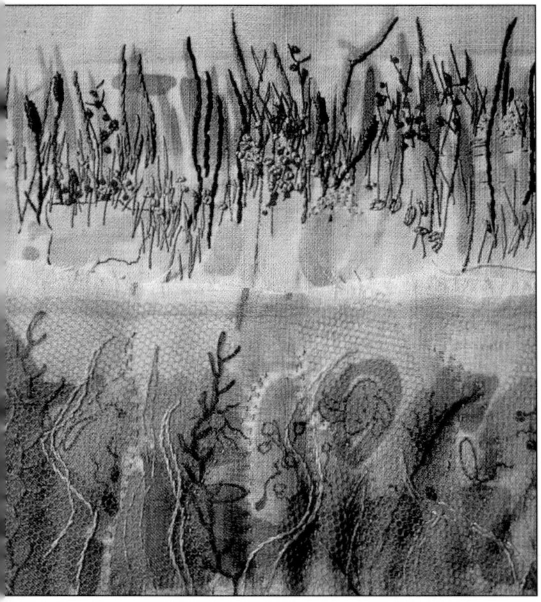

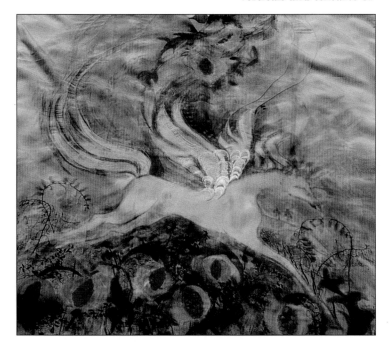

FIGURE 120. OVERLAID TRANSFER PRINTS ON FABRIC

FIGURE 121. A DETAIL OF THE *PEGASUS CAFTAN*, WITH TRANSFER DYE USED FOR A SOFT EFFECT

the printed weeds will lend themselves well to straight stitching, enhanced perhaps by tiny knots or blobs to suggest seeds, thorns, or buds. Whipstitch is excellent for blending and enriching colors, since two colors can be worked at once. For a lighter stitch effect, match either top or bottom thread to the color and value of your fabric.

Color can be used strategically to accent the focal point. Suggest flower heads, close-up or at a distance; spring leaves on trees can be scumbled in lightly with an open zigzag, moving the fabric rapidly for wide, open spacing. Don't cover the painted areas heavily, but allow them to play an important part in the composition. Try for a pleasing relationship between the color-printed fabric and the embroidery (fig. 120). I think you'll find this an exciting challenge!

Evaluate your work when you feel the stitching is completed. Note the differences in color between your painted elements and the printed. Does your stitching enhance rather than overpower the printed areas? What ideas does this generate for future pieces?

A softer, more illusionary effect of transfer dye is illustrated in the *Pegasus Caftan* (fig. 121). Here the misty, magical flying horse was painted with transfer dyes on newspaper, then transferred by warm iron to sheer polyester fabric, which lent its own qualities to the fragile, ephemeral quality of the idea (fig. 122).

I accidentally used a steam setting for the transfer and the iron left a faint pattern of holes, which added further to the ephemeral design of the flying horse. I have often used newspaper for this sort of transfer when large pieces of paper were required, and have never had any problem with the print marking the fabric. But again, I recommend a test run in

FIGURE 122. A FAINT PATTERN LEFT BY THE STEAM IRON CAN BE SEEN AT UPPER CENTER ABOVE THE WINGS.

every case. Variables in inks, fabrics, and heat do occur.

On page 14 is a detail of a long vest, *London Mews*, showing applied black cats. Figure 123 shows the reverse of that vest. Here London architectural elements, red buses, and cat figures are painted with fabric dyes directly onto the fabric. The entire piece is quilted with cat forms—horizontal, reclining cats form the cobblestones of the street on which the buses run, vertical cats rise above the painted and quilted city skyline. This is a simple, direct approach to painted dyes, quite in contrast with the misty, impressionistic effect of the previous examples.

There is no one way in which to use these paints and dyes. Once more, experimentation coupled with imagination is the key.

PRESSURE RESISTS: DISCHARGE DYEING

In discharge dyeing, color is *removed* from the fabric rather than being added to it. The process is a simple one and calls for materials that one probably has around the house: laundry bleach and white vinegar. The technique is most successful on pure cotton fabrics.

The exciting element in discharge dyeing is due to the difference in fabrics. It is impossible to predict results since most dark fabrics have a variety of dyes underneath, and unusual color combinations can emerge with the bleaching. The assorted methods of applying bleach also add to the random quality of the resultant designs, further adding to the challenge for the creative stitcher.

When bleach was brushed onto the navy blue shirt in figure 124, the resultant color was a nondescript "flesh" tone. In an attempt to make the color seem intentional, I opened up areas of the fabric and worked the openings with needle lace. The experiment worked.

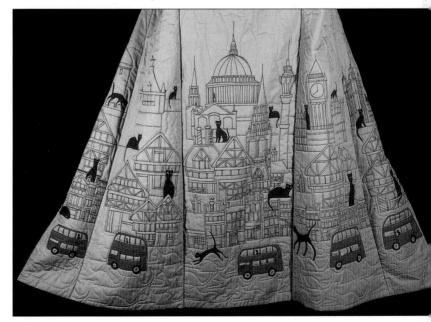

FIGURE 123. THE REVERSE SIDE OF THE VEST, *LONDON MEWS*, FEATURES ELEMENTS PAINTED ONTO THE FABRIC WITH DYES.

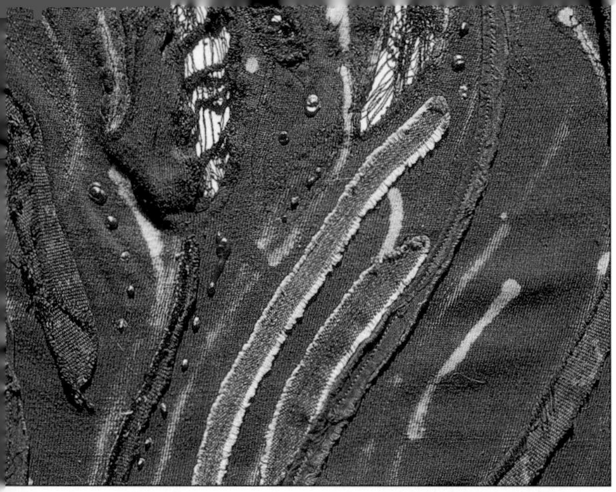

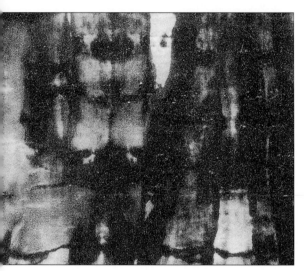

FIGURE 124. FOR THIS KNIT SHIRT, DISCHARGE DYEING PROVIDED A BASIS FOR FURTHER FABRIC ENHANCEMENT.

The flesh tones show through the lace, bringing the bleached lines and blobs into harmony with the rest of the garment. In addition, I added strips of raveled, manipulated, faded denim (the shirt was to be worn with jeans and denim skirts). Touches of copper squeeze paint suggest rivets used on jeans.

Earlier in this chapter we experimented with wax resist using paint and dye for batik. With discharge dyeing, pressure resist provides textural changes by preventing complete bleach penetration. Pressure can be achieved in a variety of ways. Fabric can be tied at intervals in tight knots. Sections of fabric can be crumpled up and tied tightly with string. Clothespins can hold clumps of fabric. Fabrics can be crumpled, pleated, and gathered with hand or machine stitches.

Figure 125 shows a piece of green velvet on which bleach was painted directly. Figure 126 is a piece of dark commercially printed cotton; figure 127 shows the front of that fabric after it had been crumpled, pleated, machine stitched, then dipped in bleach. The reverse of the piece is seen in figure 128. Figures 129 and 130 show the same fabric on which bleach was randomly brushed with no pressure at all. As you can see, each piece is completely different from the other, and all discharged pieces are eminently compatible with machine embroidery.

To machine stitch fabric for pressure resist, use a long basting stitch and the presser foot to compress the layers of crumpled fabric.

FIGURE 125. BLEACH WAS PAINTED DIRECTLY ONTO VELVET FABRIC.

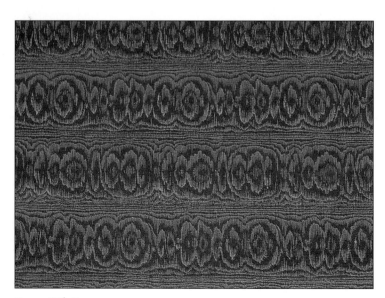

FIGURE 126. COMMERCIALLY PRINTED FABRIC, BEFORE BLEACHING

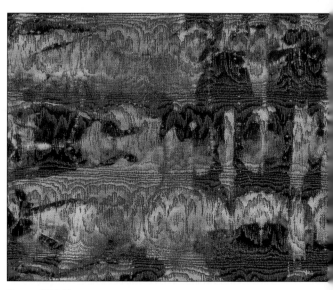

FIGURE 127. THE SAME FABRIC AFTER PRESSURE RESIST DISCHARGE DYEING

Full-strength bleach can be painted or flipped onto the fabric with a brush. It can be sprayed on with a mister. The fabric can be immersed in a plastic bowl of bleach. Be careful with complete immersion—it is easy to remove too much dye, which will reduce the strength of the pattern.

You will see the bleach working almost immediately. When the desired degree of discharge is reached, the bleach action must be stopped. Plunge the piece immediately into a bucket of water, rinse and squeeze, and place it in a bucket of vinegar solution. Allow it to remain for at least 30 to 40 minutes. Rinse under running water, then machine wash with detergent for about 10 minutes, rinse, and spin dry. Put it in the dryer. When it is almost dry, remove the stitching and/or clamps.

MATERIALS

In addition to the standard supplies, you will need: household bleach; white vinegar; ⅓ yard (.35 m) each of a variety of 100 percent cotton fabrics, dark values, some printed, some plain, some napped and/or textured; inexpensive sponge brushes; squeeze bottle or mister; buckets.

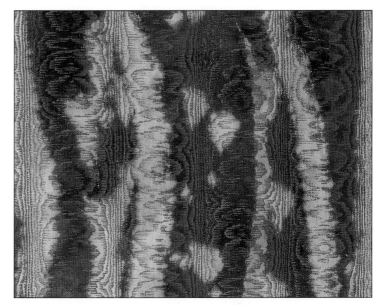

FIGURE 129. THE SAME FABRIC, THIS TIME WITH BLEACH BRUSHED DIRECTLY ONTO IT

FIGURE 128. THE REVERSE OF THE FABRIC SHOWN IN FIGURE 127

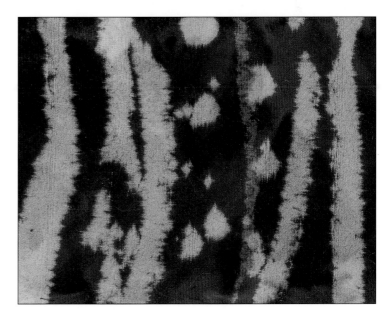

FIGURE 130. THE REVERSE SIDE OF THE FABRIC SHOWN ABOVE

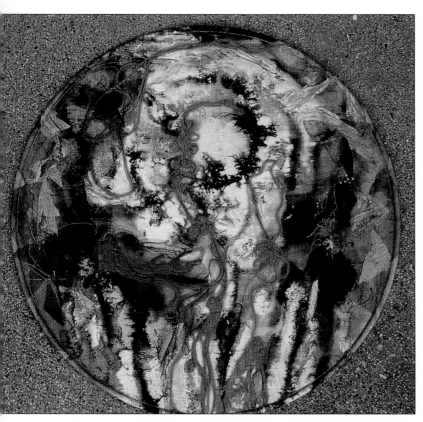

FIGURE 131. IN *RAINCROW MORNING*, ACRYLICS WERE PAINTED ONTO WET MUSLIN.

■

SAMPLER 11

EXPERIMENTS WITH DISCHARGE DYEING

Since a good deal of washing and rinsing is necessary to stop the bleaching action, the laundry room is an ideal place to work. Spread a thick pad of newspapers on the work surface, and always wear protective cover—bleach is powerful stuff! Have at hand a bucket of clear water, and a bucket of vinegar solution containing one part vinegar to three parts water.

Assemble a variety of cotton fabric pieces approximately 9 by 12 inches (23 by 30 cm). Make a series of experimental discharge-dyed fabrics, using different methods for applying the bleach, and involving different lengths of time for the discharge. On some of the pieces, try different methods of pressure resist by

stitching and clamping the fabric. Work the other pieces flat, painting, spattering or dotting the bleach onto the fabric with a brush, spraying with a mister, and stenciling. Make notes on procedure for each piece.

As each piece is finished, stop the bleach action as described above. Put pieces through the washer and dryer, and remove pressure materials. Note the methods, comment on the results, and file these pieces in your notebook.

■

SAMPLER 12

DESIGNING FOR DISCHARGE DYEING

Make another piece of discharged fabric or use several of the ones above, both front and back sides, to create a composition. Include cutting, rearranging, piecing and/or appliqué and couching, combined with selective areas of machine embroidery. Evaluate your results for your notebook.

FIGURE 132. *RAINCROW MORNING*, DETAIL.

There is a wealth of new dyes and paints on the market, and more are on the way. We may well be overwhelmed by this embarrassment of riches. My suggestion is to experiment with as many different products as your budget and needs dictate. We have set the pattern for experimentation in the exercises above. But don't feel deprived if you work only with crayons, acrylics, and ink. What matters ultimately is what you, the artist, *do* with these delightful materials.

In one of my favorite pieces, *Raincrow Morning* (fig. 131), only acrylics were used to change the surface of the muslin fabric. It is worth examining closely. Black and brown acrylics were painted onto wet muslin, creating a variety of textured areas (detail, fig. 132). Areas of darker values were enhanced by overlays of black tulle (fig. 133). Linear motions were accented by manipulating and couching strips of muslin (fig. 134) and soft acrylic yarn (fig. 135). Most of the stitching

FIGURE 134. MANIPULATED STRIPS OF FABRIC AND HEAVY THREADS ADD LINEAR INTEREST.

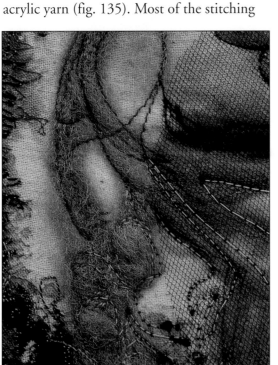

FIGURE 133. BLACK TULLE OVERLAYS ENHANCE DARKER AREAS.

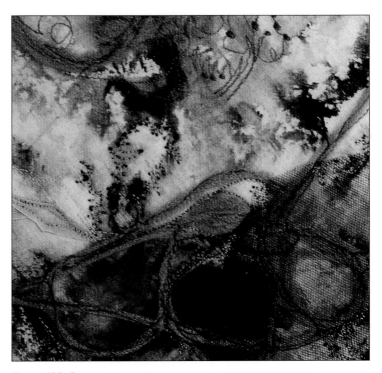

FIGURE 135. COUCHED SOFT ACRYLIC YARN PROVIDES TEXTURAL CONTRAST.

Adding Surface Color

FIGURE 136. LINES OF WHIPSTITCH END IN KNOTS AT UPPER LEFT.

was done in varying degrees of whipstitch (fig. 136) creating textured lines of light and dark threads, augmented by thicker lines of zigzag (fig. 137). A focal point was established slightly above left center (fig. 138) through a circular area strengthened with some heavy couching and black on brown stitching. This weight was contrasted with areas of delicate knots combined with whipstitch, resulting in an almost beaded texture (fig. 139). I feel this is a successful piece of embroidery, yet only the simplest of stitches and surface color were used. Selective simplicity in a piece such as this can come only after lots of experimenting to find out what fabrics, threads, and paints can do for you. It's an unending joy!

FIGURE 138. CIRCULAR MOTION PROVIDES A FOCAL POINT.

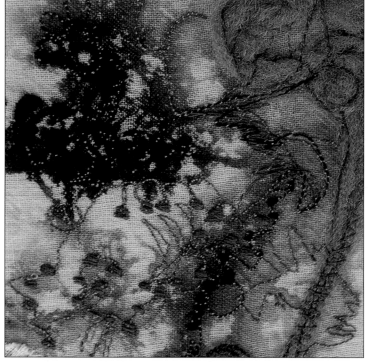

FIGURE 137. GREATER TEXTURAL INTEREST IS CREATED WITH VARIED STITCHING LINES AND THE ADDITION OF BLOBS.

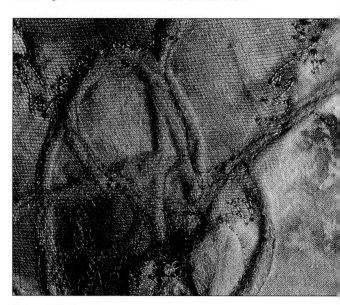

FIGURE 139. COUCHED CORDS CONTRAST WITH KNOTS AND BEADLIKE WHIPSTITCH.

Chapter 5 ILLUSIONS: PLASTICS, SHEERS, LAYERS, AND POLYMER CLAYS

HAVING LIVED ALL my life in the Midwest, a first visit to Florida left me unimpressed: broken plastic; bushes gone wrong, masquerading as trees; a place where old cars came to die. Happily, this first dreadful impression was dispelled with a closer look. I made an important discovery. The area offered an illusion that was much more significant and exciting than its reality. The limitless depth and breadth of the surrounding water combined with the intensity of sunshine and air to create a very special dimension for the senses. Our neighboring Lake Michigan provides another kind of environment, water and air with different qualities, changing seasons, the gossamer magic of moonlight and starlight, and the mists over our Skokie marshlands, all together suggesting quite different illusions of space, depth, and emotional impact.

In a sense, all art involves some illusionary interpretation of the artist's world, reflecting an emotional reaction to what is seen and felt and experienced. Embroidery often comes much closer to illusion than to reality. After all, contrary to what some dedicated stitchers might believe, the world is not made exclusively of fabrics and threads. In this chapter we shall explore some ways in which special illusions can be created through fabrics and threads, as well as some additional materials not usually thought of as embroidery supplies.

PLASTICS: ILLUSIONS OF LIGHT, AIR, AND SPACE

Plastics are often-maligned products of a synthetic, man-made age. They can be only that, but they can also serve as an exciting and creative vehicle for imaginative embroiderers. They are elements for admitting light and air to what might otherwise be a heavy, opaque piece of fabric. They can provide a light, transparent support for threads and stitches, which become much more important when a ground fabric is optically not there. And they can be used in conjunction with fabrics and threads to create a dimension of depth, distance, moonlight glow, and wetness.

Plastic handles differently from fiber fabrics. The weight and firmness of plastic make a hoop unnecessary, which allows for more freedom in stitching. On the other hand, you will find that surface tension is increased to the extent that an ordinary presser foot sometimes sticks to the surface. A teflon-coated foot can be helpful for regular stitching. For free machining, the spring-shank darning foot has a tendency to stick, but the spring needle completely eliminates the problem. Obviously, plastic does not fray or ravel, but it is stiffer and more unwieldy than fiber fabrics although it does soften a bit with working. Then there is the added challenge of transparency. The stitches acquire an additional dimension that is especially noticeable when you work over raised objects. A transparent ground also means that the reverse must be finished as neatly as the right side. It all shows!

MATERIALS

In addition to the basic supplies, you will need ½ yard (.5 m) each of lightweight and medium-weight plastic, the kind sold for use as protective table coverings or paint drop cloths; assorted odds and ends of plastics, including berry boxes, plastic curtain rings, plastic mesh bags (meant to contain oranges and grapefruit); 1 yard (1 m) black nylon tulle; waxed paper; a 5-inch (12.5-cm) metal ring; 1 yard (1 m) twisted cord.

PLASTIC AS TRANSPARENT SUPPORT

The first few exercises will be experiments in creating random design elements for working with plastic.

SAMPLER 1

STITCHING ON PLASTIC

Cut a piece of medium-weight plastic, 7 by 10 inches (18 by 25.5 cm). Set your machine for free-motion stitching, and use the spring needle. Since the plastic is quite firm and stable, a hoop is not necessary. Plan and stitch a composition using a variety of couched heavy threads in conjunction with free machining in straight and zigzag stitches. At intervals, cut slits in the plastic, allowing the heav-

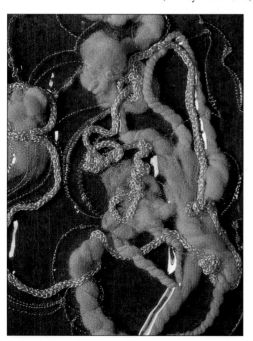

FIGURE 140. KNOTTED COUCHING AND SIMPLE STITCHING ARE WORKED ON PLASTIC.

ier threads to be pulled through to the opposite side (fig. 140). Is your embroidery as interesting on one side as the other? What sort of finished piece could take advantage of this double-sided element? What new challenges did you encounter in working with the plastic? Jot down your observations of this exercise and include them with your sampler.

SAMPLER 2

PLASTIC WITH ACRYLIC PAINT

Cut two pieces of lightweight plastic, 7 by 10 inches (18 by 25.5 cm). On one piece, paint simple areas of color with acrylic paints in harmonious colors. Apply the paint fairly heavily, and add a few drops of water here and there.

Place the second piece of plastic on top of the first, carefully matching corners and edges. Now, tilt the plastic sheets, manipulate them with your fingers, and move the paint and water drops around until you have created an interesting design. You will find that air bubbles form between the plastic layers, which

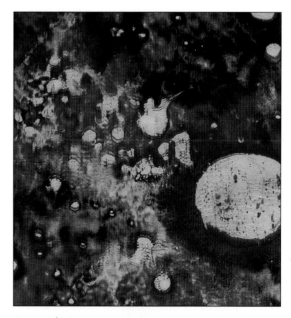

FIGURE 141. PAINT AND WATER DROPS ARE MANIPULATED BETWEEN LAYERS OF PLASTIC, THEN LEFT TO DRY.

can add a great deal to the texture and interest of the random design. When you feel the design is completed, set the piece aside on some newspaper to dry (see fig. 141).

Set your machine for free-motion stitching. With the spring needle, enhance the piece with simple stitching, emphasizing a focal point, and relating the stitching to the random design of the paint and air bubbles. Trim uneven edges, then stitch them together with a standard straight stitch or zigzag to finish the sampler.

Make notes on effects that you observed, and/or ideas for further use for this type of piece. Place both sampler and notes in a plastic sleeve in your notebook.

SAMPLER 3
PLASTIC WITH WATERCOLORS

Make another sampler, similar to Sampler 2, but this time use tube or cake watercolor. Figure 142 was painted with tube watercolors. How does the effect differ from that created by the acrylics? Is one easier to use than the other?

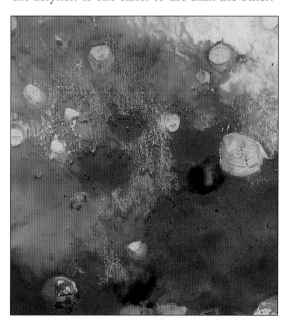

FIGURE 142. WATERCOLOR BETWEEN LAYERS OF PLASTIC

SAMPLER 4
PLASTIC AND INDIA INK

Make yet another sampler similar to 2 and 3, but this time use black India ink (see fig. 143). Comment on differences and record your observations for your notebook.

FIGURE 143. INDIA INK AND SALT BETWEEN PLASTIC LAYERS

SAMPLER 5
PLASTIC AND CRAYONS

Prepare two more sheets of plastic as above. On one piece, shred crayon bits with a vegetable peeler or sharp knife and arrange a design in your choice of colors. Sprinkle some drops of water here and there on the plastic. Carefully place the second piece of plastic over the first. Microwave for a few minutes, watching closely, until most of the crayon is soft and is beginning to melt. At intervals, manipulate the soft colors to create an interesting design (fig. 144). Notice the difference in melting in those areas where water drops were sprinkled. This should give you ideas for con-

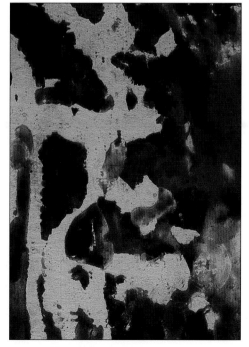

FIGURE 144. CRAYON BITS WERE PLACED BETWEEN LAYERS OF PLASTIC, THEN MICROWAVED.

trolled textural variety. Take notes, and finish the piece as above for your notebook.

SAMPLER 6
PLASTIC AND FOUND OBJECTS

Prepare two sheets of lightweight plastic as above. On one, arrange plastic bits and pieces—rings, clear sequins, beads, pieces of berry boxes. Add your choice of color medium from those used in the above exercises. Place the second piece of plastic over the first. Put the piece carefully on a sheet of paper, then on a cookie tin. Heat in an oven set at 250 to 300 degrees. Check periodically. You will find that as the plastic warms, the layers fuse temporarily, trapping the found objects in little "cages" (fig. 145).

When adequate fusion has taken place, carefully remove the piece. With the spring needle and free machining, stitch cautiously around the found objects to secure them and add stitching to enhance the design. Part of the fun of this technique is that some of the beads and small bits will continue to move inside their cages, adding actual motion to the piece. Finish the edges (as above), note comments on what you have learned, and mount in your notebook.

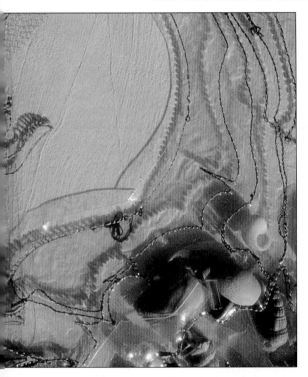

FIGURE 145. FOUND OBJECTS ARE FUSED BETWEEN LAYERS OF PLASTIC AND LATER STITCHED IN PLACE.

Blue Moon, figures 146 and 147, is a combination of paint and manipulated water bubbles between plastic, combined with aluminum foil

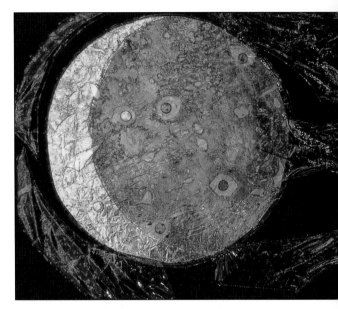

FIGURE 146. *BLUE MOON*, PLASTIC LAYERS WITH PAINT, WATER BUBBLES, AND ALUMINUM FOIL

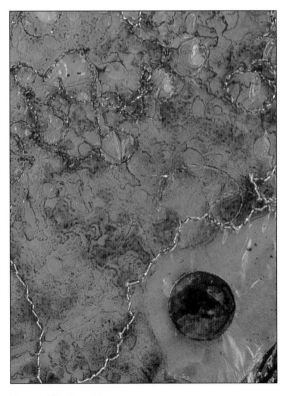

FIGURE 147. *BLUE MOON*, DETAIL

and overlaid with transparent food wrap. Simple stitching enhances the composition and fastens it to a fabric-covered foamcore board.

The lower two pendants shown in figure 148 were stitched on plastic. The green one is a section of berry box; the white is a combination of plastic curtain rings and cross sections of plastic soda straws. In each case the plastic bits were placed between two layers of water-soluble film. Stitches were worked carefully by walking the needle over the plastic edges to create embroidered patterns similar to needle lace. After stitching, the film was washed away. The top pendant was worked on tulle.

Foamcore board is another form of plastic not often associated with stitchery. But it can be useful. I have stitched plastic compositions directly to a sheet of foamcore, creating at the same time a mount for later framing (fig. 146). Figure 149 shows simple stitching on plastic on top of foamcore. Matching thread becomes almost invisible, resulting in an interesting pattern of holes in the board. In figure 150, a piece of foamcore was painted with India ink and salt. Simple stitching could enhance the varied textures of this piece. Caution: all stitching on foamcore board must be done with a presser foot in place and feed dog teeth up. Free machining is not possible; the needle simply becomes embedded in the foamcore, and breaks.

FIGURE 149. STRAIGHT STITCHING ON FOAM-CORE BOARD

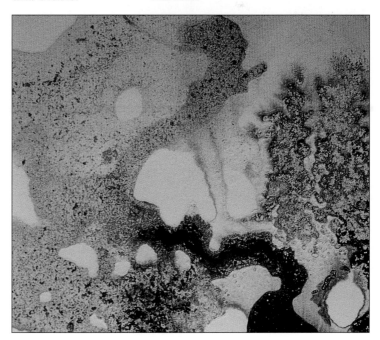

FIGURE 148. EXPERIMENTAL PENDANTS, ALL STITCHED ON PLASTIC

FIGURE 150. INDIA INK AND SALT ON FOAMCORE BOARD

Illusions: Plastics, Sheers, Layers and Polymer Clays

FIGURE 151. EARRINGS MADE OF METALLIC FABRIC THAT WAS STITCHED BETWEEN PLASTIC LAYERS

The earrings in figure 151 were made with bits and pieces of metallic fabrics placed between two layers of plastic. Random, free-machine stitching enhances the shapes of the fabric bits and secures the fabric between the plastic layers. The simple, geometric shapes of the earrings were then cut from the piece and the edges stayed with a thin line of white glue. At this point I sometimes enhance the jewel-like effect by adding dots of metallic squeeze paint. These earrings are so light in weight that the paint actually functions as an essential stabilizer as well. Finally, a hole was punched at the top for the jump ring and ear wire.

An illusionary work-in-progress piece is *The Four Seasons*. It comprises four separate plastic panels and, as this is written, three are completed. The object is to create the four panels to hang one in front of the other, so they can be changed in sequence according to the current season. Since they are worked on transparent plastic, a composite view of all four is possible. The challenge here is to plan each panel in such a way that it will harmonize with each of the others in all possible sequences. It's a fascinating compositional problem.

Winter (fig. 152) is portrayed by one large tree worked in heavily textured needle lace, both attached and detached. The root pattern extends down below the surface of the snowy ground, which is white stitching worked on manipulated white acrylic paint between two layers of plastic, after the fashion of Sampler 2.

Spring is represented by two trees, one almost bare, with a suggestion of tiny green leaves, the other in flower. Small spring flowers bloom below in a lawn of green and blue net between plastic layers. Clear plastic at the bottom allows the snowy texture of winter to show through, a reminder that the snows of winter can linger on into early spring. When the spring panel is placed on top of winter, the two smaller spring trees fall on either side of the larger winter one, their branches forming an interesting pattern of positive and negative areas.

The third completed panel, *Autumn*, (fig. 153), also involves two trees. This time, they are positioned to add to the forest effect when the three panels are overlapped. Fall foliage is suggested by whipstitched leaves worked on melted crayon slivers between plastic, as in Sampler 5. Furrowed fields are indicated in the foreground by contoured lines of open zigzag. The furrows lead downward toward areas of green, brown, and orange net between plastic, that suggest pumpkins in the field. In Summer,

FIGURE 152. *THE FOUR SEASONS*, WINTER DETAIL

the trees will have leafed out, and flowers will bloom in the foreground.

Figure 154 shows a composite of *Autumn, Winter*, and *Spring*. In the photograph the three panels were placed one on top of the other, with no space between. Even in this position there is a suggestion of space and third dimension. The illusion will be further enhanced when they are placed approximately ½ inch (1.5 cm) apart in the final arrangement. The panels will be hung from clear plastic rods suspended in a supporting frame. This way, the panels can be rearranged in seasonal sequence. The work is designed to sit on a table rather than to hang on a wall; in effect, it's a piece of sculpture.

FIGURE 154. COMPOSITE SHOWING THREE OF THE FOUR SEASONS

LAYERED SHEERS

We have explored some of the special ways in which plastics contribute to a feeling of space, depth, light, and air. You have seen how stitches and fabrics seem suspended in air, contributing to the importance of the stitches themselves. Another device which I use a great deal for creating illusions is layers of tulle.

Tulle is similar to net, but finer in mesh, and usually available in a greater color range. Silk tulle is elegant and wonderful to work with. It is made in a vast color range, but is quite

FIGURE 153. *THE FOUR SEASONS*, AUTUMN DETAIL

plex arrangement of areas and lace fillings, but is representational rather than abstract.

Another transitional piece is *Flora's Shadow*, figures 156 and 157. This is a much larger piece than the Varkie and involved a good deal of hoop repositioning during the course of stitching. The piece was inspired by a large plant that has been growing in our bathroom for years. I was particularly fascinated with the pattern that developed on the heavy stalks of the plant each time an old leaf dropped off, and by the shadows cast by the new leaves emerging at the top.

This piece was worked on a double layer of water-soluble film. It made use of old nylon hose and tulle, in combination with free machining. Patterns of lace were developed on both the fabrics, and on the film alone. The piece is stitched to a 23-inch (58.5-cm)

FIGURE 155. *THE DANCING VARKIE*, SHEER FABRICS AND LACE FILLING

expensive and may be difficult to find. Nylon tulle is inexpensive and readily available, and made in a pleasing array of colors. Either kind is relatively strong, and will not fray or ravel. Both work well in conjunction with other fabrics.

Tulle provides an element of fragile support for other fabrics, for paints, and for stitching. It holds fabric collages in place until stitching can be added, it adds important value and textural changes in all types of stitching, and it can be used for toning down the blatant strength of metallic fabrics and threads. Used in conjunction with multicolored fabrics, it adds a soft, subtle patina that suggests the special richness of antiquity.

The Dancing Varkie, figure 155, is a transitional piece between the lace and openwork of Chapter 3 and the illusionary use of sheers in this chapter. It shows an aardvark dancing with an ant, and adds not only a more com-

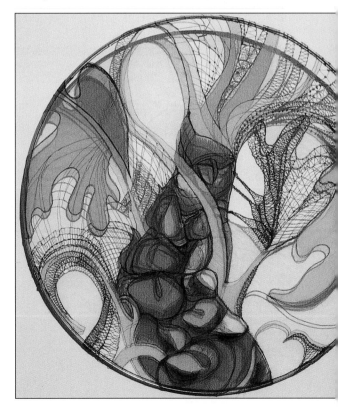

FIGURE 156. *FLORA'S SHADOW*, A GRACEFUL COMBINATION OF NEEDLE LACE AND SHEER FABRICS

FIGURE 157. FLORA'S SHADOW, DETAIL. NOTE THE USE OF BLOBS IN THE LACE FILLINGS.

brass ring, then mounted on small transparent posts 1 inch (2.5 cm) above a larger circle of fabric-covered foamcore. The raised mounting allows shadows from the embroidery to be cast on the neutral ground, creating further patterns of fragile leaf designs. The illusion of light and shadow changes continuously with the shifting light of the day.

MATERIALS

You will need an assortment of sheers: 12-inch (31-cm) squares of tulle, nylon hose (get a three-pair packet of colored knee-highs at the local discount store), net, and organdy; bits of plastic as used for Sampler 6; water-soluble film; four 8- or 9-inch (20- to 23-cm) metal rings for mounting.

A COLLAGE OF SHEERS

We shall begin with a circle of vegetable bag mesh and assorted sheer fabrics. Place the outer ring of a 10-inch (25.5-cm) hoop on a table and place the mesh over it. Lay one of the metal rings on this to determine the area of the composition. Arrange a collage of sheers related to the mesh, some overlapping, and all suited to the circular format of the ring. Decide where the focal point will occur. Think in terms of which spaces will be fabric, which will be lace filling, and which will remain completely open.

When an interesting pattern of sheers, positives, and negatives is achieved, remove the metal ring and place a piece of film over the entire composition. Carefully secure it all with pins. Place the inner hoop in position and frame the piece for free machining. With a paint pen marker (see page 53), indicate which areas are to remain as mesh, which will be open, and which will be lace filled.

To maintain the necessary tautness of the fabric, we will cut away and stitch just one area at a time. Begin with the established focal point and work outward in all directions, alternately cutting and stitching from there toward the perimeter.

Begin by cutting away the fabric from one design area. Work from the wrong side, taking care to cut the fabric only, leaving the film intact. If you should accidentally cut the film, just pin another piece in place underneath. Stitch this area, securing the edges and/or filling it with a pattern of lace. As you work, gently tighten the fabric in the hoop, as it tends to relax as more areas are opened up. Continue this process of opening areas, stitching, and developing the composition until the entire piece is stitched.

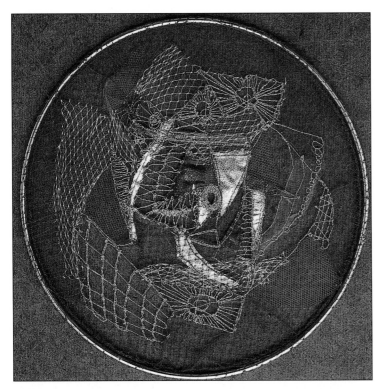

FIGURE 158. A COLLAGE OF VEGETABLE BAGS, TULLE, AND METALLIC FABRICS

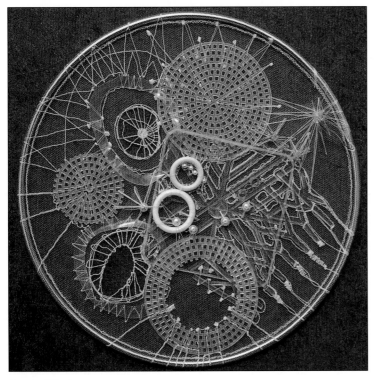

FIGURE 159. AN ILLUSIONARY COLLAGE

Remove the embroidery from the hoop and mount on a metal ring (see page 58). Wash away the film. Evaluate the delights and challenges of this piece, and jot down notes for your notebook.

For the piece shown in figure 158, I used mesh bagging in two colors, net, tulle, and pieces of metallic fabrics. Some of the stitching was worked in metal threads.

SAMPLER 8
WORKING WITH TULLE

In this exercise we will combine white or light-colored tulle with an assortment of transparent or translucent plastic found objects: berry box sections, plastic soda straws, six-pack rings, plastic needlepoint canvas, curtain rings, beads, and any other appealing bits (fig. 159).

Place a 12-inch (30.5-cm) square of tulle on top of the outer embroidery hoop ring. Arrange on it a collage of plastic objects. Some should be raised, such as cross-sections of plastic straws, standing on end, and several layers of clear plastic berry box parts. Establish a focal point, and suit the shapes of your collage to the circular area for which you are designing. Cover the finished collage with a layer of water-soluble film and pin carefully, making sure that the raised items are properly upright. Insert the inner ring of the hoop to frame for free machining.

Use a combination of simple free machining and spanning threads (shown in the drawing on page 65) to secure the found objects and enrich the transparent patterns of plastic shapes. Mount the finished piece on a metal ring, dissolve the film, and assess your results. Notice, particularly, how various stitches react with the raised areas, and the illusion of depth that is created by this elevation.

OVERLAPPING SHEERS

This sampler explores the value changes that occur when sheers are overlapped and layers cut away. You will need at least three close-valued sheers. White organdy, eggshell or beige tulle, and light, flesh-toned nylon hose would be ideal for creating a monochromatic value-oriented composition. Since nylon hose fabric has a good deal of stretch, I find it easiest to work on an ironing board, where it can be temporarily pinned in place.

Put the outer ring of the hoop on the ironing board, and over it place a 12-inch (30.5-cm) square of organdy and of tulle. Carefully stretch the hose section over the top and pin it to the board. Over this place a piece of water-soluble film, insert the inner hoop, and frame for machining. Place a mounting ring on the piece, inside the hoop, and draw around it to mark the circumference of your composition.

Plan a design on the film using the paint marker pen. Establish a focal point and design areas that work well within the prescribed circle. Some areas will be cut away entirely, some will be filled with needle lace, and some will be cut out only partially, revealing different levels of fabric. In this way, value changes will be established that will add variety and illusionary depth to the piece (see fig. 160).

Work in the same cutting/stitching sequence described for Sampler 7, working from the reverse side and leaving the film intact. One, two, or all three fabric layers can be removed. As you work, gently adjust the fabric to keep it taut in the hoop.

Mount this piece on a metal ring. In areas

FIGURE 160. A MONOCHROMATIC COMPOSITION OF OVERLAPPING SHEERS

where the fabric does not extend to the ring, stabilizing spanning threads and patterns of needle lace should be walked over the ring in order to support the composition when the film is removed (see page 65).

Hold the piece to the light to make sure that all edges are secured and firmly supported. Then dissolve the film. Repair any dangling threads or unsupported edges that might have escaped your notice.

COLORED SHEERS

In sampler 9 we worked with value changes and multiple layers of monochromatic sheers. In this exercise we shall carry the idea a step further and work with multiple layers of different colors, changing not just value, but the

FIGURE 161. SHEER LAYERS OF COLORED NYLON ARE ADDED IN SOME PLACES, CUT AWAY IN OTHERS.

colors change as layers are removed. Small pieces of nylon can be added if a different color sequence is needed. As you stitch, play with this concept of adding and subtracting, changing colors and values. Develop an interesting composition of varied layers, open space, and needle lace (fig. 162).

There is no right or wrong side to a piece like this. Hold it against the light to test colors and values, and notice how the scheme varies from one side to the other. When it is finished, mount it on a ring. Make sure that all areas are adequately supported, then dissolve away the film.

Just for fun, hang these last four samplers in a window. Does this give you any ideas for using them in future embroideries?

Multiple layers are particularly effective for soft jewelry. Blatantly glitzy fabrics, threads, and glitter paint can be used, then toned down with a covering of one or two layers of tulle so that only a subtle, gem-like glow

colors themselves (fig. 161). The process is an additive as well as subtractive one. Layers will be cut away in some areas and added in others. For this we will use the colored nylon stockings.

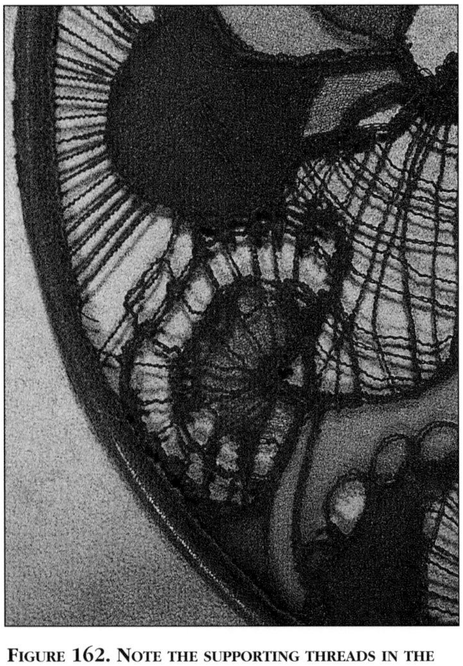

Pin layers of colored nylons over the outer rim of the hoop and notice how the colors change as one is added on top of another. Add a layer of film, and draw a design on it as for Sampler 9. Begin the stitching and cutting away procedure, taking into consideration how

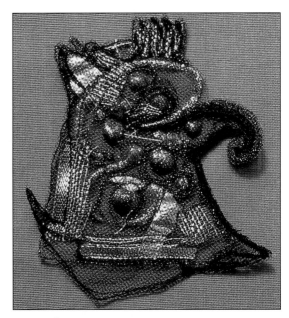

FIGURE 162. NOTE THE SUPPORTING THREADS IN THE COMPOSITION OF COLORED SHEERS.

FIGURE 163. A PENDANT FEATURING A STYLIZED GRYPHON COMBINES PAINT WITH NYLON TULLE.

Illusions: Plastics, Sheers, Layers and Polymer Clays

remains. The layers of sheer create wonderfully rich effects.

The pendants in figures 163 and 164 were made by squeezing paint onto a layer of nylon tulle. Since some paint does ooze through the tulle, I worked on a piece of waxed paper (foil doesn't do). After the paint dried, beads, sequins, and fabric bits were added, and the whole was covered with another layer of tulle. The double layer of tulle was then framed in a hoop for free machining. The stitching not only secured the objects, but enhanced the designs these elements suggested. Edges were finished with multiple rows of straight stitch.

One of the delights of working with this technique is collecting all those bits of glitter and glitz that we all secretly wish we could use, but we don't quite know how to avoid producing something resembling a cross between

FIGURE 164. THIS PENDANT INCORPORATES PLASTIC SODA STRAWS, PAINT, AND TULLE; IT'S STITCHED WITH METALLIC THREAD.

a carnival prize and a Las Vegas chorus girl's costume. I had great fun collecting lengths of metallic ribbon; small scraps of fabrics (all synthetics, usually very cheap); iridescent wrapping "paper" in colors that resemble those of soap bubbles and is impervious to water; beads; sequins; metallic yarns; twisted paper ties; and a range of squeeze paint in iridescent, metallic, and glittery colors.

The initial inspiration for all this was, I think, attendance at gem shows with our daughter, who is a goldsmith and jewelery designer. My mind boggled at the myriad colored gems, tables filled with strings of moonlight-glow pearls, miles of textured gold chains. The senses ached from the sheer stimulation of it all! So, I, who had shunned anything glittery for many years, found myself wallowing in the pure delight of working with an exciting clutter of glitz.

WRAPPED CORDS

Basically, all jewelery can be reduced to either cords (including strings of beads, ring bands, and chains), or pendants (settings), all of which simply become our familiar lines and areas. It is easy to wrap cords on the machine. and they provide harmonious support for pendants, beads, and other stitched and jewelled areas.

The white lace collar shown on page 67 is supported in this way. For it I used ¼-inch (7-mm) jute cord, but a woven or braided cord could be substituted. Use the spring-shank darning foot with feed dogs down. Stitch up and down in place into the cord two or three times to lock the stitches, then set the machine for a wide zigzag and stitch back and forth as you slowly and steadily pull the cord through under the needle.

Practice to develop an even, steady pull, and

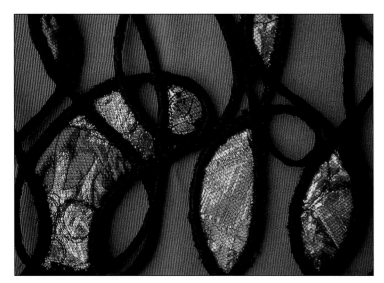

FIGURE 165. BRACELET, WITH METALLIC FABRICS AND WRAPPED CORD

yards of the stuff as prom decoration, then tossed it into the dumpster. One never knows where these goodies will turn up. The main thing is to keep your eyes open, and hoard your glitzy collection for that time when the gem and jewelery urge comes upon you.

I have experimented with a variety of colored tulles, and find that black, brown, and navy are most effective for my purpose. Lighter tints seem to water down the colors underneath, rather than enriching the effect. Brown and navy are more difficult to find, so black is probably the best beginning color.

SAMPLER 11
SMALL PENDANTS

We will begin by making a few small pendants, suitable for earrings, brooches, or elements of a necklace. Place a sheet of waxed paper on a cookie tin, and cut two notebook-sized pieces of black tulle. Place one piece on the waxed paper. With squeeze paint in the colors of your choice, create a number of small, freeform designs, using the paint primarily as dots of jewel-like color. The paint is most effective in blobs and larger areas, which complement the linear nature of machine embroidery.

Enhance these small designs with bits of fabrics, beads, sequins, metallic cords—whatever strikes your fancy. Pieces can be overlapped, built up in multiple layers, and in the case of the transparent, iridescent paper, can be placed on top of other fabrics and over blobs of paint. When you are satisfied with your designs, cover the entire area with the second piece of tulle and allow the paint to dry overnight.

When the paint is dry, frame the piece for free machining, and enhance the designs with stitchery. Gold and silver threads work well here, heavier cords can be couched, and stitched knots and blobs relate well to the

the wrapping will be smooth and will completely cover the cord. Straight stitch in place several times to finish off the wrapping. The bracelet detail in figure 165 was constructed of this kind of cord, doubled back on itself and stitched into convoluted curves to create lines and areas in a freeform design. Metallic fabrics were added as fillings to suggest the effect of gems set into a mounting. Purchased cords or chains can be used effectively to support pendants. It all depends upon the effect that you, the designer, wish to obtain.

As for the pendant areas, this is where the real fun begins. You won't need much of any one thing, but variety and multiplicity of colors are vital. Spend a few days, or more, simply browsing in crafts shops, fabric shops, hardware stores, and stationer's stores.

Treasures are everywhere. A wonderful bonus was once sent to me packed around a birthday gift—shredded iridescent packing material that was almost as welcome as the gift it protected. Another time, my husband came home after an early morning run with a bushel basket of iridescent soap bubble "paper." A local college had evidently used jewel-like areas of paint. Delineate the shapes of the individual designs with two or three concentric and closely spaced lines of straight stitching, relating this to the colors in the individual designs. This stitching not only marks the shapes of the pieces, but provides a slightly stiffened edge to add stability when the area is cut out.

If you wish to use these small designs as earrings or pendants, stitch a circular area at the top into which a jump ring (and ear wire) can be inserted. For a brooch, fasten a purchased pin back on the back as part of the stitching. Several of these pendant pieces could be joined as shown and worn as a necklace or jewelled collar.

Carefully cut just outside the edging lines; the tulle won't fray. Wear your distinctive jewelry with pleasure, or file the pieces in a partitioned plastic sleeve along with your comments.

The method described is a basic one for making individual units of jewelled designs. The more you work with them, the more ideas will

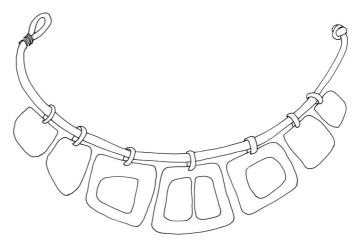

FIGURE 167. A SERIES OF SMALL PENDANTS CAN BE SLIPPED OVER A LENGTH OF WRAPPED CORD TO MAKE A NECKLACE OR COLLAR.

be generated for incorporating them into innovative pieces of wearable art. If you plan to use them as decorative motifs on a garment, be sure to test your materials first for washability. I have found that most of the metallics and plastics hold up well in water, but test runs are always a good idea.

Figure 168 shows a detail from a shirt that was designed using units of this sort of fabric/paint collage.

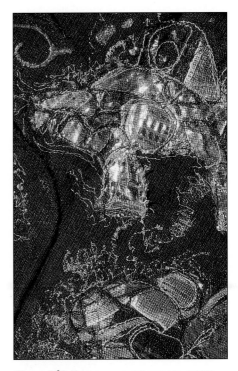

FIGURE 168. FABRIC AND PAINT COLLAGE, DETAIL FROM A SHIRT

You can see how the tulle not only holds the small bits and pieces in place for stitching, but it also serves to tone down the tawdriness of some synthetic fabrics and threads, and enriches the entire piece. Double-needle pin-tucking further relates the stitched to the non-stitched areas.

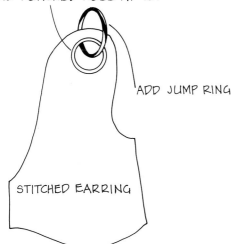

STRAIGHT STITCH TWO OR THREE TIMES AROUND PUNCHED HOLE AT TOP

ADD JUMP RING

STITCHED EARRING

FIGURE 166. REINFORCE THE HOLE AT THE EARRING TOP WITH SEVERAL ROWS OF SHORT STRAIGHT STITCHES CLOSE TO THE FABRIC EDGE.

Figure 169 also shows a detail from a shirt. Here, additional layers of net were applied and manipulated to create value changes and to serve as a transition between the heavily embroidered areas and the negative areas of the garment.

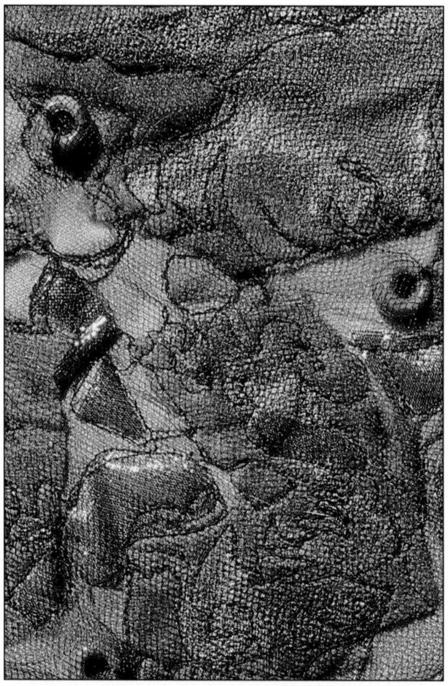

Fig. 170 shows a pin (the smallest circle) and two pendants, all of which make use of illusionary materials to create an atmosphere or environment. The smallest, *Starburst*, began as a fabric collage on black percale. It includes bits of metallic fabric, strips

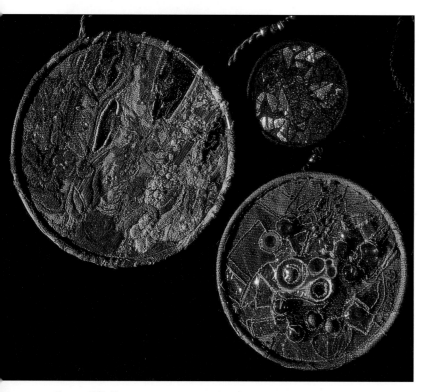

FIGURE 169. PAINT, ENCAUSTIC, AND METALLIC FABRICS UNDER MANIPULATED TULLE

FIGURE 170. THE SMALL PIN AND TWO PENDANTS ARE EXAMPLES OF ILLUSIONARY SOFT JEWELRY.

of gold packing material, and tiny metal stars.

All were framed in a hoop under a piece of black tulle; free machining with dark brown thread accented the patterns of fabric and secured all pieces. Dark brown stitching on black enriches the fabric color and prevents it from looking dead. An alternative is to use brown or navy tulle over black fabric.

After the stitching was finished, a 2¼-inch (5.7-cm) metal bangle was placed over the composition and free-motion satin stitch was worked carefully over the bangle to finish the edge and anchor the stitchery to the ring. Excess fabric was trimmed away, then a second row of zigzag was worked over the bangle. A bar pin back was stitched to a piece of felt, and the felt glued to the back.

The medium-sized circle features a thin cross section of a shell, combined with beads, metallic fabric pieces, iridescent paper, and various overlays of tulle, arranged in such a way as to create subtle value changes. Tulle was placed over the composition. Stitching, in brown and a variety of green threads, was added to enhance the design. The entire piece was mounted on a 5-inch (12.5-cm) metal ring. Beads and a knotted cord (support for the pendant) were stitched in as the mounting took place, and a circle of felt was glued to the back.

Pendant Garden, the largest of the three circles, is a more complex version of this type of pendant. An impressionistic flower garden is suggested by arranging a collage of small fabric bits on a green percale ground. As you can see, there is no one way to combine these elements into impressionistic, illusionary embroideries, suggesting space, light, and air.

SAMPLER 12

A PENDANT GARDEN

The object of this exercise is to create a wearable, illusionary garden (see fig. 171). The illusion will be built of tiny pieces of printed and plain fabric in a wide range of color and values. The greater the range, the richer the effect. Multiple layers of fabric bits can be used. For this you will need a 6-inch (15-cm) metal ring, 10-inch (25.5-cm) squares of black and green tulle, a 10-inch (25.5-cm) square of felt in a color related to the piece, and 1 yard (1 m) of twisted cord to support your pendant.

As a guide, choose a favorite garden photograph—your own or from a magazine. Study it carefully to see how many colors and values are involved; there will be more than you think. What are the dominant verticals and horizontals? Where will the focal point occur? Where do you see light and space between the plant forms? How do these relate to the individual plants? Choose a basic ground fabric. If both ground and sky are involved, piece the ground fabric to create that effect.

Place the metal ring on the ground fabric and trace around it with chalk to define the size of the pendant. Using tiny pieces of fabrics, create a fabric collage, building up an impressionistic garden, carrying some pieces beyond the circumference of the circle. Values are extremely important. Try to create the feeling of depth, space, and air in your garden.

Place the square of green tulle over the entire composition. Pin carefully in a few places to prevent bits from moving too freely; some movement under the needle is desirable. Frame in a hoop. Stitching should be fairly simple since the scale is small. Secure the main verticals and horizontals first, then, with

a rotary cutter or very sharp scissors, carefully slit (do not cut out) and manipulate the open places for lace. Cut through both the green tulle and the ground fabric; the slits will contribute to the vertical illusion of stems.

FIGURE 171. WEAR YOUR COLORFUL GARDEN!

Use both hard and soft edges to create textures of stalks and stems (fig. 172). If more stability is needed at this point, back the openings with tightly stretched water-soluble film. The spring needle is advisable here. More fabric bits can be added as you work.

Remove the piece from the hoop, back the entire piece with black tulle, and reframe. Re-chalk the perimeter of the circle and develop the remainder of the stitching

FIGURE 172. OPEN SPACES IN THE "GARDEN" SUGGEST SPACE, LIGHT, AND AIR.

FIGURE 173. *THE SEASONS TURN, RENEWING AS THEY CHANGE*

For the neck cord, determine the length of cord necessary to hang your pendant at the length you prefer, and add 1 inch (2.5 cm). Be sure the cord will slip over your head. Measure approximately 2½ inches (6.5 cm) around the ring in both directions from the top center, avoiding the lace openings, and pin the cord at these positions. Spread the fibers apart at the cord ends to prevent unsightly bumps. Stitch each end in place close to the ring, allowing ½ inch (1 cm) to remain free. Trim the ends and secure the fibers to the back of the pendant with a touch of white glue.

Mark the perimeter of the ring on the felt square, and free-stitch your signature on the felt, avoiding the lace openings. Cut the circle of felt to fit inside the ring on the pendant back. Mark the lace openings and carefully cut them out. Position the felt and lightly glue it to the back of the piece, covering the glue-secured ends of the cord. Wear your pendant garden with joy—this one will never need weeding!

A different manifestation of the *Pendant Garden* technique is a large two-module piece, *The Seasons Turn, Renewing As They Change* (fig. 173). Each season is worked on the same principle as Pendant Garden, combining fabric collage, slit and manipulated fabrics, and layers of sheers to suggest not only space and atmospheric conditions, but to further the notion that each season contains reflections and vestiges of the previous one (fig. 174). The two-seasons modules are fastened together with hook and loop tape.

I remember as a child admiring illustrations for bridal gowns, traditional long, satin gowns with gracefully trailing lace—romantically called "illusion lace." Just the name conjured up magic and hidden wonders. Illusion lace

beyond it. This allows for judicious cropping and repositioning of the final composition. Leaves and flower forms can be extended onto the black tulle, adding to the spacial effect of the stitching. I find that a light whipstitch with green thread in the bobbin and flower colors on top creates a soft blending of flower tones with foliage. When stitching is completed, remove the piece from the hoop and wash away the stabilizer. Dry, and mount on the ring (page 58).

this next project is not, but in a sense it is illusionary for it involves layers, and the putting together of a number of techniques that create space and depth. It combines appliqué from Chapter 1, fabric manipulation from Chapter 2, lace and openwork from Chapter 3, and the stabilizing sheers described above.

For want of a better label, I call the process illustrated in figs. 175 and 176 "pencil lace," because a pencil is used to stabilize the fabrics and threads as they are stitched. A crocheted web is added, then manipulated and distorted as the stitching progresses. This lace is particularly effective for wearable art, for soft jewelry or elements applied to a basic garment. An entirely new fabric is created that provides three different ways in which a ground fabric or the wearer's skin tone can show through

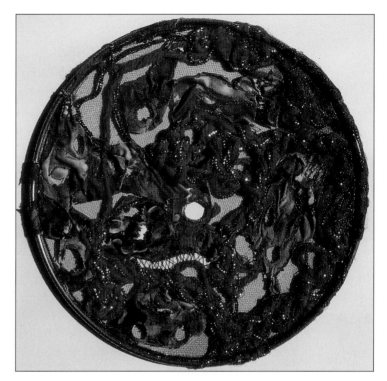

FIGURE 175. A SAMPLER OF "PENCIL" LACE VARIATIONS

the lace. Some areas are cut away completely; some are cut out and filled with needle lace. Others are darkened by the tulle to provide a subtle value and tonal change in the underlying hue, be it skin tone or the color of the garment underneath. Aesthetically, this is an important unifying element in creating a complete, harmonious effect.

FIGURE 174. *THE SEASONS TURN*, DETAIL

FIGURE 176. DETAIL OF PENCIL LACE SAMPLER

SAMPLER 13

CROCHETED COLLAGE

Crochet a very open, irregular web as illustrated, using two different kinds of thread. In the piece shown in figures 175 and 176, one strand of soft acrylic yarn and one strand of rather crisp metallic cord were used. Make three or four irregular pieces in this manner.

Candle (see page 43) pieces of 100 percent nylon or polyester printed fabric in colors related to the crochet threads. Place a 14-inch (35.5-cm) square of water-soluble film on the table and outline the circumference of the 9-inch (23-cm) circle on it. Place two layers of tulle on top. On the tulle, arrange a fabric collage of the crocheted webs and the candled fabric pieces, their edges extending at least 1 inch (2.5 cm) beyond the perimeter of the circle in all directions. Pin the pieces in place.

Plan this composition to include a focal point and pleasing relationships of positive and negative spaces. The positive areas are the threads

FIGURE 177. AN OPEN, IRREGULAR CROCHETED WEB PROVIDES THE FOUNDATION FOR PENCIL LACE.

and fabrics. The negatives include some areas to be cut away completely, open areas to be filled with needle lace, and other places where only the tulle will show.

Carefully frame the three layers, gently pulling the fabrics taut, but being careful not to tear the fragile tulle and film. The stitching is relatively simple, and at times becomes completely obscured by the textures of the lace. Use only enough stitching to secure the elements, allowing as much texture to rise above the ground surface as suits your composition. I used primarily straight and whip-stitches with a few blobs for contrast.

As you stitch, support the area directly around the needle with the point of a pencil from which the point has been broken off, or with a cuticle stick. A great deal of stability is required when so many different layers of fibers are involved. As you progress, use the pencil to pull and distort the loosely crocheted web, shaping interesting areas of positives and negatives as you stitch. When the stitching is completed, remove the piece from the hoop and mount it on a metal ring, following directions on page 58.

Dip the piece in water to dissolve away the film, and allow it to dry. During this time you can determine which areas should be completely cut away, which should be filled with lace, and which should remain simply as tulle.

When the piece is completely dry, use small embroidery scissors to cut away those areas you wish to be open. Work needle lace fillings in some of them (see page 64). Since the metal ring serves as a hoop, no further framing is necessary for working the lace, but do support the threads with your pencil. Why doesn't the spring needle or the spring-shank embroidery foot work for this technique?

FIGURE 178. A PENCIL LACE COLLAR

The collar in figure 178 was worked in this same way, using a modification of the collar pattern described in Sampler 16. The yarn, used doubled, was a thin, tightly twisted, variegated thread with intermittent slubs that added considerably to the interesting texture of the piece. Beads were incorporated to lend

jewel-tone texture as well as additional weight at the bottom of the collar (fig. 179).

Figures 180 and 181 show a cropped top that was made from the same threads, to be worn over a specific shirt and matching pants. The openings in the lace relate the top beautifully to the remainder of the garment and complete a unified outfit.

It is interesting to note how completely different figures 176 and 181 are, yet they are made exactly the same way. It is a graphic example of how different threads can create an entirely different fabric.

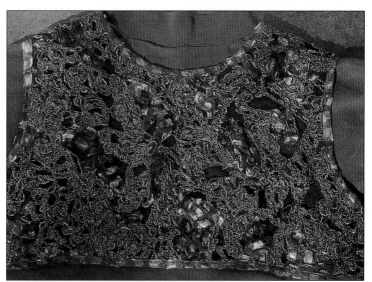

FIGURE 180. A CROPPED TOP WORKED IN PENCIL LACE

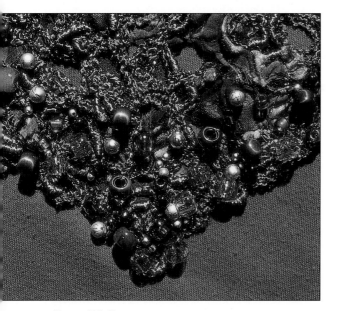

FIGURE 179. BEADS ADD RICHNESS, TEXTURE, AND WEIGHT TO THE BOTTOM OF THE COLLAR.

FIGURE 181. THE OPENINGS IN THE LACE ARE IMPORTANT IN RELATING THE TOP TO THE GARMENT WORN UNDERNEATH.

THE ILLUSION OF ANTIQUITY

In the previous material we've been dealing with illusions of light, air, and space. Illusions of antiquity are equally challenging. I've always been fascinated with artifacts and archeological excavations. Ancient textiles and jewelry have a luster and patina that only time can bring. One year in London, I bought an old piece of Indian embroidery (fig. 182), stitched in intricate patterns with metal threads and highlighted with shisha. The entire piece was overdyed, subduing the once brighter colors, and contributing to the soft luster of the metal threads.

FIGURE 182. OVERDYED ANTIQUE INDIAN EMBROIDERY

Several years ago an historic production of Wagner's *Ring Cycle* was performed on television on four successive days, the only time it has been done the way in which Wagner envisioned. I was impressed with the characterization of Brünnhilde by Hildegard Behrens and was tremendously moved by the strength and drama of the entire performance. I wondered what her battle-scarred shield would have looked like after surviving the heat of Loki's magic fire and the final inundation by the Rhine. Surely it was a beautifully wrought bronze shield, skillfully chased, and set with precious stones. Remnants of the magic fire and the blue-green water of the Rhine must have lurked in its depths, combined with the patina and deterioration of untold ages. *Brünnhilde's Shield, After the Immolation* (fig. 183) was the product of this experience.

FIGURE 183. *BRÜNNHILDE'S SHIELD, AFTER THE IMMOLATION*

On black percale I combined crayon encaustic, which suggested the patina of weathered bronze, gold, silver, and copper squeeze paint, many layers of metallic fabric mosaics, and a few beads. On top are layers of iridescent plastic and black tulle. The metallic fabrics,

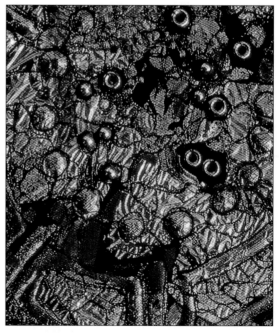

FIGURE 184. PAINT, LAYERS OF METALLIC FABRIC, AND BEADS WERE USED IN THE SHIELD.

covered by the iridescent plastic, suggested the inner flames still a vital part of the magic shield (fig. 184).

Stitching includes straight stitch, zigzag, whip, and knots and blobs. Threads are black, brown, and several tones of bronze-greens to suggest ancient metals. Warm colors form the focal point in the center of the shield, then become gradually cooler toward the outer rim. Some areas, primarily toward the outside perimeter, were slit and either edged with satin stitching or folded back and straight stitched, allowing some of the gold-colored mounting ring to show, relating it closely to the gold paint and metallic fabrics used toward the center of the shield (fig. 185). The piece is mounted on a 23-inch (58.5-cm) ring.

This experimental impressionistic piece, combined with long hours spent in museums and galleries, inspired a series of embroideries which I call artifacts. I have attempted to suggest the ancient patina and soft metallic luster of old embroideries and of antique jewelry pieces that have been excavated from historical burial sites. I developed a series of soft jewelry and shields that incorporate crayon encaustic, multi-layers of metallic fabric bits, squeeze paint, and beads. The glitz is subdued with layers of iridescent plastic and tulle.

FIGURE 186. AN ARTIFACT COLLAR, A CUFF, PINS, AND PENDANTS

SAMPLER 14
ARTIFACT COLLAGE

Select a 12-inch (31-cm) square of dark-hued percale or similar fabric. Print random patterns on it with crayon encaustic. Iron the fabric between layers of newspaper to set the colors and remove excess wax (see page 69). Add some jewel-like dots of squeeze paint. Gold is always good, as are intense ruby red, emerald green, and sapphire blue. Allow the paint to pile up quite heavily to suggest precious stones. Let it dry overnight.

Develop a collage on the encaustic with small bits of metallic fabrics. Concentrate on establishing a focal point and a pleasing relation-

FIGURE 185. NEEDLE LACE SUGGESTS FABRIC DAMAGED BY TIME.

ship between the added fabrics, the encaustic patterns, and the negative space of the plain fabric. By using small pieces, some overlapping, a mosaic effect can be created. Overlay the mosaic with pieces of iridescent plastic, if you wish, to bring about color changes with changes of direction and light.

Finally, cover the entire collage with a layer of black or brown tulle and frame for free stitching. Using primarily straight stitch, delineate the edges of the fabrics and paints, breaking the areas into a variety of small mosaics pieces. Add some whipstitch and blobs to relate to the changing colors and the painted "jewels" (fig. 187). Whipstitch with multicolored threads not only adds richness, but adds a raised texture to suggest the mosaic matrix.

To further the impression of antiquity, slit selected areas of fabric, particularly toward the perimeter of the circle, turn back some edges and stitch them into the texture of the piece. Other openings can be satin stitched with a variety of subtly colored threads that lead naturally into the overall pattern of stitches (fig. 188). A mix of colored threads, both top and bobbin, contributes a great deal to the impression of rich antiquity.

When stitching is complete, mount the piece on a metal ring (see page 58). If your ring is gold colored, you will find that where sections of the ring show through the fabric slits, an important connection between the mounting ring and the gold paint is established, adding to the unity of

FIGURE 187. THE STITCHING SUGGESTS GROUT LINES IN THIS FABRIC MOSAIC COLLAGE.

your composition (fig. 185). The choker and collar in figure 190 were made of multilayered fabric mosaics.

SAMPLER 15

AN ARTIFACT CUFF

For this exercise, use the cuff from a commercial blouse pattern, or make a pattern of your own: Position a piece of paper around your wrist or arm and mark the desired length and width. A wider cuff should taper slightly

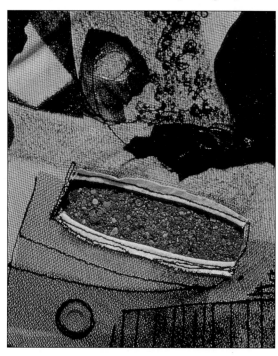

FIGURE 188. FABRIC EDGES CAN BE TURNED BACK AND STITCHED.

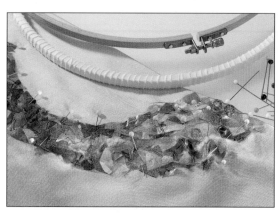

FIGURE 189. A FABRIC MOSAIC COLLAR IN PROGRESS

toward the wrist to follow the contour of your arm. Allow 1 inch (2.5 cm) at each end for overlap, and add ⅜ inch (1 cm) seam allowance on all sides.

With a chalk marker, outline the pattern on a piece of percale in the color of your choice. Stitch around the pattern with monofilament thread to mark the edges on both right and wrong sides. The stitching will not be noticed after construction. Use the pattern to cut a cuff facing from the same fabric or one that harmonizes with the colors of your planned design.

Create a multi-layered mosaic as in Sampler 14. This time, locate the largest pieces of mosaic at the center of the cuff—the focal point—and gradually diminish them in size toward the ends. For a cuff, do not slit the fabric. Cover with a layer of tulle, pin in place, and carefully frame in the hoop for stitching. As above, plan the stitching to further the impression of grout between mosaic pieces.

Sign your name on the right side of the facing, along the center. Place the cuff face down on the right side of the facing and pin in place. Stitch carefully around the edges, following the monofilament stitching line, and leave a 3-inch (7.5-cm) opening at the center of the upper long edge for turning. Trim seams to ¼ inch (.5 cm) and carefully clip corners and outside curves.

Turn the faced cuff to the right side, using a point turner or bodkin to gently poke each corner to a proper point. Run a ruler along the inside edges of the long seams to make sure they are completely spread apart. Press gently from the wrong side, then topstitch around the edges of the cuff with matching thread. This makes a firm, nicely finished edge. Stitch two pieces of matching hook and loop tape at each end of the cuff, overlapping 1 inch (2.5 cm) to form a closure. Wear your cuff with pride!

FIGURE 190. A COLLAR AND CHOKER MADE USING FABRIC MOSAIC TECHNIQUES

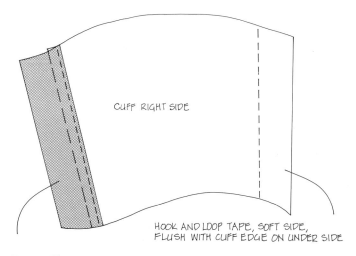

CUFF RIGHT SIDE

HOOK AND LOOP TAPE, SOFT SIDE, FLUSH WITH CUFF EDGE ON UNDER SIDE

HOOK AND LOOP TAPE, HOOK SIDE UP, EXTENDED BEYOND CUFF EDGE

FIGURE 191. ADD A HOOK AND LOOP TAPE CLOSURE TO THE FINISHED CUFF.

SAMPLER 16
AN ARTIFACT COLLAR

The collar is made in the same way as the cuff. Create a pattern for it from a basic dress pattern with a neckline that falls where you wish your collar to sit. My collar tapers in width from approximately 4½ inches (11.5 cm) at center front to 1 inch (2.5 cm) at the back closure. Any shape, regular or irregular, can be planned for the collar, but as a first exercise a simple shape will be easier. Variations can be developed later.

Print a piece of fabric with melted crayons, add squeeze paint and

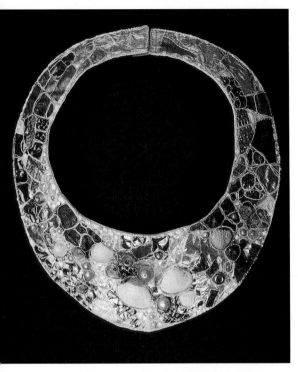

FIGURE 192. SHELLS INCORPORATED INTO A FABRIC MOSAIC COLLAR

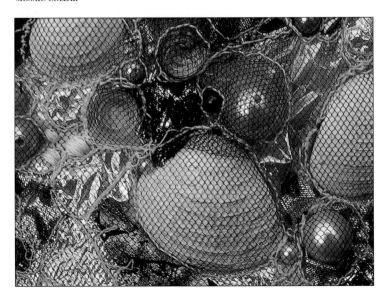

FIGURE 193. SHELLS AND BEADS ARE COUCHED IN PLACE UNDER TULLE.

the multilayered mosaics of metallics and transparent materials. Keep in mind that the more small pieces of harmonious colors you combine, the richer and more jewel-like will be your effect.

Allow the paint to dry overnight. Develop the mosaic, cover with tulle, then frame and stitch it. Construct it as you did the cuff. In the blue collar, figures 190 and 187, dark, jewel-like colors were combined with gold paint to create an opulent effect.

In figure 192 the sea-toned mosaics were combined on white fabric, and shells were stitched in under the tulle to create the illusion of an undersea scene. Although the stitching was done with off-white thread, I used black tulle on top (fig. 193).

A similar collar was worked on white fabric covered with pastel pink tulle, stitched in pastel greens, blues, and violets. Crystal beads and clear sequins added to the iridescent, icy impression of this one.

ILLUSIONS OF WATER AND DEPTH

We have been working at creating illusions of light, air, space, and antiquity. Another fascinating challenge occurs in creating the illusion of water. Water seems always changing, due to environmental differences. It can be stormy or calm, shallow or deep, soothing or menacing, realistic or fantastic. I've long been fascinated with the story of the flood that is part of many ethnic histories, most notably in the story of Noah and the ark. (We collect arks in our family.) The cycle of cataclysm and redemption, the promise of the rainbow, and the repetitive motif of pairs of animals provide rich material for many forms of design, and most certainly for stitching.

FIGURE 194. *THE 39TH DAY*, DESTRUCTION AND THE PROMISE OF HOPE

The 39th Day (fig. 194) is one manifestation of this fascination. Here dramatic changes in values (the dark, stormy skies and surface of the flood in figure 195, contrasted to the lighter values of the very deep water where a drowned city lies) are suggested by layers of sheer tulle, thick and thin satin-stitched lines,

and heavily textured couching. The fury of the storm is suggested by change of scale—the very large bolts of lightning contrasted with the tiny ark (fig. 196), almost enveloped by the roiling waves.

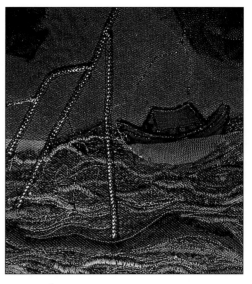

FIGURE 196. A CHANGE OF SCALE ADDS DRAMA.

A variation on this theme is *There Be Unicorns* (fig.197). The unicorn, modeled from polymer clay, is seated on a raft, towed by the ark just disappearing at right. Rough, dark seas are suggested through combinations of needle lace, heavy couching,

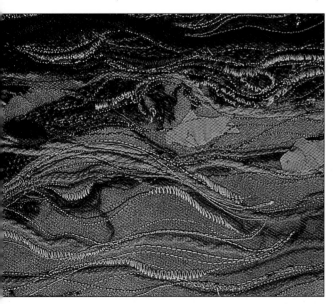

FIGURE 195. STORMY SEAS FROM *THE 39TH DAY*

FIGURE 197. HEAVY COUCHING INDICATES THE WAKE OF THE ARK. THE UNICORN IS POLYMER CLAY WITH COUCHED YARN.

Illusions: Plastics, Sheers, Layers and Polymer Clays

and multiple layers of sheers (fig. 198). The white body of the unicorn directs the eye to the upper left of the composition where a subtly glowing rainbow arc bears the legend, "There be unicorns."

This stylized and fantastic concept was suggested by a medieval map of the world I once saw in London. Where the Pacific Ocean would

FIGURE 198. HEAVY COUCHED YARNS ARE USED TO SUGGEST HEAVY SEAS IN *THERE BE UNICORNS.*

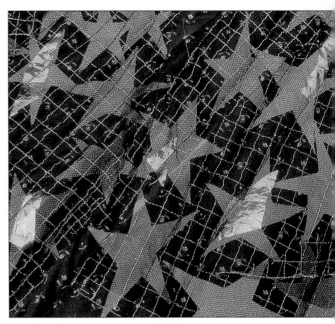

FIGURE 200. IN *MOLLY'S QUILT*, NETS OF SILVER AND GOLD NEEDLE LACE ARE CAST TO CATCH THE "STAR FISH."

have been, the ancient cartographer drew fantastic creatures, further identified in beautiful calligraphy, "Here there be dragons."

In quite another vein, *Molly's Quilt* (fig. 199) represents Eugene Field's children's poem, *Wynken, Blynken, and Nod*. Here the illusions are several. Not only is the sea (the nighttime sky) suggested, but all the magic of dreams is there—shimmering moonlight, stars as fish, gold and silver nets, and the imagination of childhood (fig. 200). Iridescent plastic is layered under sheers to create the illusion of a gossamer sail, and stars are entangled in a net of machine lace worked with metallic gold and silver threads. Freeform quilting in combination with appliqué suggests both wave motion and a shimmering corona of moonlight (fig. 201). The entire quilt is surrounded with a border of applied and quilted wave motifs.

In figure 202, *Nofretete Worships Ra*, an illusion of third dimension occurs. The large, circular wall panel began as a stylized Egyptian collar. The pointed elements rotating around

FIGURE 199. *MOLLY'S QUILT:* THE SEA, THE NIGHTTIME SKY, THE MAGIC OF DREAMS

the center opening are a combination of applied fabric and block printing. I cut simple triangles from foamcore board and printed them with metallic squeeze paint (fig. 203). But as I worked, I realized that not only was the collar beginning to resemble a sunflower, but the dark center was obtrusive, blank, flat, not really related to the idea of either a collar opening or a flower center.

Pondering the problem, I realized that the Egyptian collar/sunflowers idea could combine. Greek myth tells that the sunflower worshipped the sun god, Apollo, keeping its face turned toward the god as he drove his flaming chariot across the sky. The Egyptian sun god is Ra, and Nofretete, the beautiful queen of early Egypt most certainly wore a collar similar to the one pictured here. Hence the title, which alludes to both ancient cultures.

Striving for further suggestion of antiquity, I candled a doubled piece of black tulle, sprayed it lightly with gold, and positioned it partially across the offending central area. This change solved the relationship problem, eliminating the completely flat center, and it created an

optical illusion which seemed to bring that central area up and toward the viewer, producing a strong three-dimensional effect.

FIGURE 202. *NOFRETETE WORSHIPS RA*, A WALL PANEL IN THE STYLE OF AN EGYPTIAN COLLAR

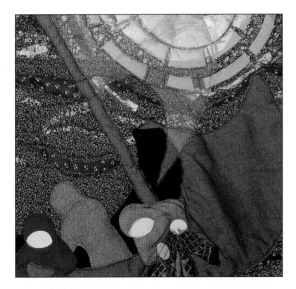

FIGURE 201. FISHERMEN HAUL IN THEIR NETS AND MOONLIGHT GLOWS THROUGH A GOSSAMER SAIL.

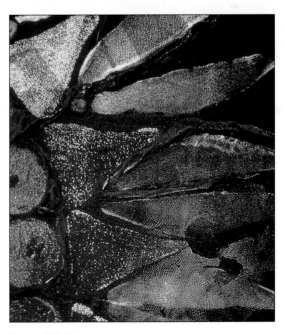

FIGURE 203. BLOCK-PRINTED ELEMENTS ARE SUBDUED WITH TULLE.

POLYMER CLAYS

In the Introduction I mentioned actual and implied volume, and we have been working with the latter in these last few exercises. By way of contrast, and fun, let's explore an entirely new aspect of actual volume through the use of polymer "clay." This is an ideal medium with which to work and to relate to embroidery and fibers in general. It is easy to handle, it comes in many colors, it can be mixed to create new colors, it fires in a regular oven, and it keeps its shape without shrinkage. It can be painted, covered with gold leaf and bronzing powders, and it accepts photocopy transfer. It is extremely versatile and forgiving.

Much has been written on the art of polymer clay, and more is coming out all the time. Our approach to this art form is a simple one—that of a machine embroiderer relating an exciting object of our own creation to the success of the finished piece.

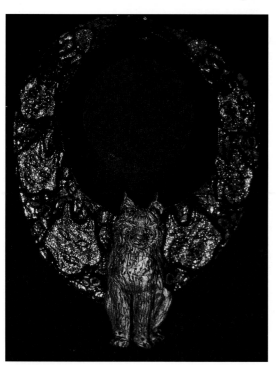

The collar in figure 204 provides a transition from mosaic collages to the exploration of polymer clays. It includes a motif of block-printed cat heads, footprints, and a lynx modeled from polymer clay. The cat head shapes were cut from foamcore board, squeeze

FIGURE 204. THE *LYNX COLLAR*, INCORPORATING POLYMER CLAY, BLOCK PRINTING, AND FABRIC MOSAIC.

paint was applied, and the prints made on fabric. The prints were applied to the collar along with the mosaics, then covered with a layer of tulle and stitched. Stitching was worked through the paint to delineate the contours of the stylized cat features The clay lynx is stitched on with threads taken through holes in the clay which are part of the pattern and texture of the cat's fur.

MATERIALS

We shall begin our polymer clay experiments by creating a "personality angel." In addition to the usual supplies, you will need the following: ½ yard (.5 m) light to medium cotton/polyester fabric, chosen to suggest your angel's personality; small pieces of color-related fabrics for appliqué and manipulated areas; several 12-inch (31-cm) squares of nylon tulle in assorted colors for overlays; a variety of color-related machine threads; heavier threads and cords for couching; a thin-bladed palette knife; assorted beads, if desired; a 9- by 12-inch (23- by 30-cm) piece of glass; a 9- or 10-inch (23- or 25.5-cm) metal ring for mounting; acrylic paints and inexpensive brush; a 65-gram block of white or near-white polymer clay.

Two good brands of polymer clay are readily available in art supply shops. One is a bit harder to prepare for working (I use a heating pad and two cats to soften it; lacking this equipment you can sit upon it for a while). This firmer variety holds detail well. The softer clay requires less kneading and preparation, but fine details are a bit more difficult to achieve.

■

SAMPLE 16

A PERSONALITY ANGEL

The nice thing about angels is that each person's idea of what one looks like is as valid as anyone else's. We use a stylized angel form because it is easily simplified, an important consideration for the first-time sculptor. The shape relates well to fiber textures, and it can express personality in a definitive way. Your challenge is to indicate that personality vividly

FIGURE 205. THIS FIGURE FROM *EVENING ANGELS FOLD THEIR WINGS IN REST* SHOWS HOW SUBTLE SHAPING OF THE POLYMER CAN SUGGEST MOOD OR FEELING.

and imaginatively. Begin by choosing and defining your angel's personality (see figures 205 and 209).

Cover a baking tin with doubled paper toweling and place the glass on it. Shape the angel directly on the glass. Knead and manipulate the clay until it is malleable and comfortable in your hands. Begin with a column approximately 5 inches (13 cm) long and 2½ inches (6.5 cm) thick; later you may remove or add material. Indent the neck area and shape a slightly oval head. Keep the shape simple; concentrate on proportion and posture.

Pinch out the wing shapes from the column, pulling and flattening the material. Shape draped folds to suggest the remainder of the body. Visualize gestures to communicate the mood of the angel—a drooping head and wings to indicate sorrow or rest; an uplifted head, thrown back, with wings soaring upward to suggest joy or excitement. The clay can be reworked as many times as necessary.

Using a heavy needle or toothpick, suggest wing contours and feathers and incorporate small holes or slits into the texture of the feathered wings and draped folds of the gar-

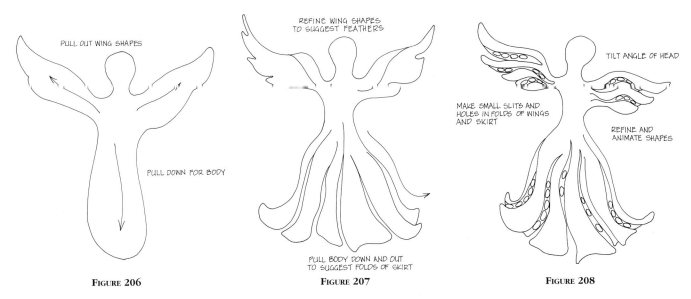

FIGURE 206

FIGURE 207

FIGURE 208

ment for stitching later. Make them an integral part of the overall design and texture of your angel. In the drawing, the holes are exaggerated in size for clarity. Make sure the size of the angel is appropriate for the metal ring.

FIGURE 209. *ANGEL OF THE RAIN*, POLYMER CLAY WITH STITCHING

Bake the figure on the glass, tin underneath, at 250 to 275 degrees for approximately 15 to 20 minutes. Ovens and clay thickness will vary, so check periodically. It should not brown, except perhaps a tiny bit around the thin edges. It will be slightly rubbery when it is first removed from the oven, but will harden as it cools. If it remains rubbery, return it to the oven to bake a few minutes longer. Run the palette knife blade gently under the clay to loosen it from the glass, then lift it clear when it has cooled.

Meanwhile, thought and preparation should be directed toward embroidering an environment for the angel. Create one that will enhance and amplify the mood and personality of the figure. Plan the layout within the circle of the 10-inch (25.5-cm) hoop. Use all or some of the following techniques: painted ground fabrics;

manipulated appliqués, multicolored mosaics under tulle; couched threads and strips of fabric manipulated to emphasize contoured areas; whip and cable stitches; needle lace overlay; beads, under tulle or strung and couched (figs. 209 and 210). You may express the mood of your angel in any way you feel directed, but don't overlook this opportunity to try new and exciting techniques.

As you plan the composition, consider where your focal point—the angel—will be placed, and work the stitching in all directions from there. Some stitching will be continued after the embroidery is mounted and the angel is in place, but painting can be done at any point. When the composition is well under way and a good deal of stitching has been worked, mount the piece on the ring (see page 58).

Determine colors for the paint wash to use on the angel; only a little pigment is needed. Mix hues on a square of foil to best suggest your angel's personality. Thin the paint with water as you work, and brush the wash on quickly, allowing pigment build-up in the low areas. Some wash can be used on the fabric and threads as well (fig. 205).

FIGURE 210. SMALL HOLES OR SLITS IN THE POLYMER ALLOW FOR STITCHING AFTER THE PIECE HAS BEEN HARDENED.

Illusions: Plastics, Sheers, Layers and Polymer Clays

Allow wash to dry, then dust with metallic paint if desired. Metallics can be applied first, allowed to dry, and the paint applied over them. With sprays, make a baffle of newspapers to prevent the paint from drifting, and work in a well-ventilated room with no pilot lights or other open flames.

FIGURE 211. *THE ARK ANGEL COLLAR*, PAINTED POLYMER CLAY WITH A PIECED "RAINBOW" SUPPORT

Position the angel where it will provide an effective focal point for the composition. To keep it in place for stitching, touch a few drops of tacky glue to the angel's back and press it onto the fabric.

To stitch the angel to the fabric, use a bare needle and carefully stitch into a hole in the clay; lock by stitching in place. With the presser foot lever raised, extend the thread to the next hole, carefully positioning the thread so it follows the contours of the clay. If necessary, using a toothpick, put a tiny dot of tacky glue in the groove to stay the thread. Stitch in place

several times to lock the stitch, then move to the next spot. Lead these threads to the edge of the clay through contoured grooves, then continue whatever stitching is desirable on the fabric. The idea is to relate this stitching to both the contours of the clay and the elements of the ground fabric.

A close relationship between fabric, threads, and clay is necessary for a successful composi-

FIGURE 212. *THE PEGASUS COLLAR* INCORPORATES POLYMER WITH FABRIC MOSAIC, CANDLED FABRIC, AND COUCHED CHENILLE ACCENTS.

tion. Since the angel is a raised element, some heavily textured couching and the addition of beads or knotted strips of fabrics all contribute to a close harmony of elements (fig. 205). Assess your piece often and critically to see if it works as a composition with a pleasing relationship between positive and negative areas. See that it suggests the chosen mood and personality of your angel. Sign your piece, hang it according to the instructions on page 59, and enjoy it.

■

This concept can be taken in many different directions. In figure 211, *The Ark Angel Collar,* rainbow patchwork comprises the body of the collar, with the ark, Mr. and Mrs. Noah, and the winged angel animals stitched onto it. *The Pegasus Collar* (fig. 212) features a large clay winged horse, symbol of poetry and imagination, combined with fabric mosaic under tulle, candled fabric, and some couched chenille threads. The wings were made separately and are not fastened to the body, leaving them free to bend and follow the contours of the neck.

The *Piasa Bird* collar (fig. 213) represents the official dragon of Illinois. In the 17th century Father Marquette, traveling along the Mississippi just north of St. Louis, saw a huge petroglyph carved into the eastern bluffs over-looking the river. It depicted a red and green winged dragon with terrible teeth and claws, and great antlers like those of a deer. For years, as legend goes, the Illini Indians lived with it in peace, until it happened during time of war to taste human flesh. From then on it preyed on the hapless Indians until a great warrior was able to kill it.

Father Marquette made crude drawings of the petroglyph, and from those drawings the leg-end continues. In my interpretation the wings are separate from the body, which, with the antlers, subtly suggests the shape of Illinois. The wings are articulated and shaped to follow the contours of the neck. Strips of red metallic fabric are woven through large openings in the wings, then pulled through and puffed in some places to provide high textural relief, and to relate with the body as well as to the fabric and couching on the body of the collar. Under the open jaws and eyes of the dragon is red foil; the pupils are tiny, faceted jet beads.

Impressions and illusions are in the eye of the beholder. They can change with the subject, the environment, the mood and background of the observer, and with the circumstances of the viewing. We are dealing with ephemeral ideas and interpretations of personal experiences. For me, this is what makes the whole concept interesting. We have explored, certainly from the standpoint of traditional embroidery, unusual combinations of fabrics, threads, and other materials. And who can say what new and fascinating materials lie ahead for the creative fiber artist?

In his 1819 poem, *Ode to the West Wind*, Percy Bysshe Shelley wrote:

Drive my dead thoughts over the universe
Like withered leaves to quicken a new birth!...
Scatter, as from an unextinguished hearth
Ashes and sparks, my words among mankind!

I hope the material in this book will, like Shelley's west wind, scatter ashes of old traditions and sparks of new ideas over your own universe so that you can experience some of the joy, the wonderment, and the headiness of exploring and learning new things that I have found in my own experiments. Remember, this is only a beginning; take these ideas and soar with them!

FIGURE 213. *THE PIASA BIRD* COLLAR, POLYMER AND FABRICS, IS MODELED AFTER A DRAGON CARVING ON THE BLUFFS ABOVE THE MISSISSIPPI RIVER.

INDEX OF SAMPLERS

GENERAL INDEX